DETERMINING TRUTH
FROM ERROR

Apostle Wendell Archie

MINDSTIR MEDIA

Published by Mindstir Media, LLC
45 Lafayette Rd | Suite 181| North Hampton, NH 03862 | USA
1.800.767.0531 | www.mindstirmedia.com

Printed in the United States of America
ISBN-13: 978-1-7344892-8-6
Library of Congress on file with publisher

Apostle Wendell Archie has preached the gospel of Jesus Christ for over forty-five years. He has successfully initiated churches in Louisiana, Texas, and Indiana, and has established a worldwide ministry through radio, television broadcasts, campus ministries, and social media platforms. He currently serves as the Apostle over seven churches in the states of Texas and Louisiana that are served by three Bishops and thirty-five Pastors. With an extraordinary determination to stay true to Bible principles, he has not been swayed by the different doctrines and popular beliefs of today's "modern" preachers. His ministry of obedience to the truth founded in God's Word has successfully freed countless people from the bonds of sin, including homosexuality, promiscuity, alcoholism, drugs, violence, poverty, anger, pride, and many others. Apostle Archie writes this book to empower the reader to see the sometimes-subtle differences between true doctrine and error. This is vitally important for a victorious life now and into eternity with the Lord. Jesus said, "And you shall know the truth, and the truth (not error) shall make you free." John 8:32

Introduction

In reading this book, you will find the key components in God's Word that will help you to become completely pleasing to God. In these last days, it is very difficult to determine truth from error because there are hundreds of different versions of the Bible. None of these different versions state the same thing. This should never be the case when it comes to God's Word. Apostle Paul said in 1 Cor. 1:10, "Now I beseech you, brethren, by the name of our Lord Jesus Christ, that ye all speak the same thing, and that there be no divisions among you; but that ye be perfectly joined together in the same mind and in the same judgment." This cannot be accomplished unless we can discern truth from error.

This book will help you to expel incorrect doctrine, traditions, and Scriptures that are misquoted or taken out of context. Scriptures that are misquoted or taken out of context are lies, even though they are quoted from the biblical text. For example, Satan spoke the Bible to Jesus, but every time he did so, he was lying *with* the Bible because his statements were taken out of context. Jesus stated it is the truth that makes you free. No man can be saved believing a lie. According to 2 Thess. 2:11-12, believing a lie will cause a person to be damned. Paul warned in 1 Tim. 4:16 saying,

"Take heed unto thyself, and unto the doctrine; continue in them: for in doing this thou shalt both save thyself, and them that hear thee." Paul also instructed in 2 Tim. 2:15 to "Study to shew thyself approved unto God, a workman that needeth not to be ashamed, rightly dividing the word of truth." This means you can speak or divide the word of truth incorrectly. You may preach the word of truth and be preaching a lie if it's not spoken in the correct context. In other words, if the word is not spoken within the context intended by God, then the entire message is false, and those that believe it are deceived.

To discern truth, it is important to know the subject and context to understand what the writer is conveying. For example, 1 Timothy and 2 Timothy were written to a young convert who had realized the call of God upon his life; he had a desire to serve God in ministry. Paul was instructing this young man on how to become a true minister. It was not by following statements of preachers or popular books written by famous ministers, which can lead to error, but rather to study the Scriptures *only* to precisely determine what the Bible is actually stating.

When the Bible is correctly understood, it will not contradict itself. No Scripture will be contrary to other Scriptures when it is understood correctly.

If there seems to be contradictions in the Scriptures, you

Determining Truth From Error

need to carefully examine the context of both Scriptures. This may be achieved by reading the whole chapter of the Scripture. Your thought of the Scripture should not vary from the entire storyline from which the Scripture is taken. It is important to know the narrative of every Scripture that you use to avoid abuse of the Scripture. If you are going to use a Scripture, you *must* keep it within the context of what was written in the Bible. It is important for you to understand what I am saying because these are tools that Satan's ministers are using successfully to trick God's people; they will quote Scriptures, but oftentimes not in the correct context. Reading this book will help you to determine truth from error.

CHAPTER 1

Lying with the Bible

Satan's Example

Satan spoke the Bible to Jesus, but every time he opened his mouth, he was lying with the Bible because the statements that he made were taken out of context. For instance, Jesus went to the mountain, and the devil tempted him in this very passage: ". . . And said unto him, If you be the Son of God, cast yourself down: for it is written, He shall give his angels charge concerning thee: and in their hands they shall bear thee up, lest at any time thou dash thy foot against a stone" (Matt. 4:6).

Here, Satan is using the Bible to tell Jesus that he can literally jump off the mountain, and before he hits the ground, the angels will come and scoop him up. But in Psalm 91, where he took this Scripture from, this is not what the Scripture was speaking about. "He that dwelleth in the secret place of the most High shall abide under the shadow of the Almighty. . . . There shall no evil befall thee, neither shall any plague come nigh your dwelling. For he shall give his angels charge over thee, to keep thee in all thy ways. They shall bear thee up in their hands, lest thou dash thy foot against a stone" (Ps. 91:1; 10-12).

Now the Scripture did say that the angels shall bear thee up, but it was speaking in terms of the enemy coming at God's people and God sending his angels to protect them. It was not speaking in terms of God's people throwing themselves off a mountain and never hitting the ground, but this is how the devil used it. Satan's ministers are using all types of teachings in this same fashion. That's why you have to study this Bible. I have observed ministers doing this often (turning the truth into a lie), and the people are rejoicing in lies because they don't study their Bible. I want to note that speaking or using the Scripture out of its context is speaking a lie.

As another example, one can justify suicide using the Bible in the wrong manner. Let me show you: ". . . And he cast down the pieces of silver in the temple, and departed, and went and hanged himself" (Matt. 27:5). Reading this truth in error, one may say, "Throw your money in the temple, go and depart out of that church, and hang yourself." This Bible quotation states what Judas did after betraying the Lord. It was not instructing anyone to do the same. A lying prophet may use the following Scripture to confirm that you should go commit suicide. Then said Jesus unto him, "Go, and do thou likewise" (Luke 10:37). Now I can take this Scripture and say to you, "Judas hung himself, now you go and do the same thing." I quoted part of Luke 10:37 lying, because it wasn't quoted in its correct context. I took the Scriptures out of context and gave them a different meaning.

I have heard ministers say, "For the grace of God that brin-geth salvation has appeared to all men," supposedly quoting Titus 2:11. Understanding this Scripture in error could appear that all men have the grace of God. When you include verses 12-14, then you will understand grace appearing to all men, but grace is rejected by most men because grace teaches that you must deny ungodliness and live a righteous and holy life in this present world (Titus 2:12-14).

Let's look at Titus to see what Paul was really talking about to get the whole understanding of it:

> "For the grace of God that bringeth salvation hath appeared to all men, Teaching us that, denying ungodliness and worldly lusts, we should live soberly, righteously, and godly, in this present world; Looking for that blessed hope, and the glorious appearing of the great God and our Saviour Jesus Christ; Who gave himself for us, that he might redeem us from all iniquity, and purify unto himself a peculiar people, zealous of good works" (Titus 2:11-14).

Grace comes to teach you how to live a righteous and godly life in this present world. It does not come in teaching it's okay to sin. Grace teaches you about denying ungodliness! Grace teaches you to deny worldly lusts and that you should live soberly, righ-teously, and godly in the world that we are now living in. Grace teaches you that Jesus will redeem you from all iniquity. Any minister who preaches to you that grace doesn't make you zealous toward doing good works is Satan's minister. To omit this from their teachings is wrong.

When you are tempted with worldly lusts, grace will empower you to refuse a sinful lifestyle. Grace teaches you to do what is right! Notice the Scripture says in this present world, meaning now—not when we all get to heaven! The majority of people love preachers that give them encouraging words only and make them feel everything is okay, so when grace is preached correctly (denying ungodliness and worldly lust) it is not understood.

The Preacher as the Problem

Many churches are growing very fast because preachers are afraid to speak about homosexuality, racism, adultery, fornication, respect of persons, drunkenness, pornography, bigotry, and hatred. They want political leaders to address all these things. Why are we disturbed at the political leaders when that is the preacher's duty? When the minister neglects to teach against these sins, the congregation doesn't leave, and they continue their support for their church but will become angry with the political leaders because they don't speak against all these things. Who are the ones responsible for this mess? These churches and their pastors are responsible for this nation's moral decline. When you get a government that is of the people, by the people, and for the people, the government is going to change its rules according to the people's minds. So, who is in charge of changing the mindset of the people? The pastors are. It is a mistake to expect moral guidance from the president rather than the pulpit. It would be good if the president were righteous, but the Bible states, "For the priest's lips should keep knowledge, and they should seek the law at his mouth: for he is the messenger of the LORD of hosts" (Mal. 2:7).

This is another misunderstood quotation, "There is therefore now no condemnation to them which are in Christ Jesus" (Rom. 8:1). The preachers don't keep reading; they stop the verse there. But the Scripture goes on to say, "who walk not after the flesh, but after the spirit." This passage clearly explains individuals who will choose a lifestyle after spiritual things rather than fleshly things; these are the people that are not condemned. It is not to all that claim Jesus as their Lord, but to those that walk as he walked. Jesus said, "Not every one that saith unto me, Lord, Lord, shall enter into the kingdom of heaven; but he that doeth the will of my Father which is in heaven" (Matt 7:21).

Have you ever tried to talk, and someone just cuts you off? When the preacher quotes part of the Scripture, they are cutting off Paul's words and the true meaning of that Scripture. It was hard for me to call these preachers Satan's ministers at first. I tried hard to think that perhaps they were just blind. But when I started to see them skillfully skip over these Scriptures and cut off parts, I saw they were doing it just like the devil does it. Anytime a preacher tells you that you can't live by the Bible or the commandments, he is doing just what the serpent did to Eve:

> *"Now the serpent was more subtil than any beast of the field which the LORD God had made. And he said unto the woman, Yea, hath God said, Ye shall not eat of every tree of the garden? And the woman said unto the serpent, We may eat of the fruit of the trees of the garden: But of the fruit of the tree which is in the midst of the garden, God hath said, Ye shall not eat of it, neither shall ye touch it, lest ye die. And the serpent said unto the woman, Ye shall not surely die: For God doth know that in the day ye eat thereof, then your eyes shall be opened, and ye shall be as gods, knowing good and evil" (Gen. 3:1-5).*

And likewise, as the serpent spoke part truth, leaving out a portion resulting in a lie, so do Satan's ministers. (The serpent did clearly say the truth that her eyes may be opened knowing good and evil. But the part about her not surely dying was a lie.) They don't negate everything that God says, but they take out the vital parts of what God is trying to say to you. I heard one of Satan's ministers say when God gave us commandments he knew we couldn't keep them. But where did God say he knew we could not keep them? What gives you the audacity to challenge what God gave his children to do? How would you feel if you told your child to study their lesson and your neighbor told your child that he didn't have to study his lesson? What if one of your siblings told your child that his parents know that he can't make an "A" in class? See, that sounds comfortable to the child. The parents know where the child is at the current time, but they are trying to teach the child to go higher. This is how the churches are today. When you are struggling in something, and you believe it is a difficult task to perform, what you don't need is a popular minister to justify your weakness by saying, "It's okay to come short of what God says." In the day of judgment, the Bible says these books will be opened, and everyone will be judged according to what is written.

"There is therefore now no condemnation to them which are in Christ Jesus, who walk not after the flesh, but after the Spirit. For the law of the Spirit of life in Christ Jesus hath made me free from the law of sin and death" (Rom. 8:1-2). This is saying that the person who is led by the Spirit of God and not by his own desires is not condemned. This Scripture explains why you are not condemned when the Spirit of God leads you. The Spirit of God is able to write all of God's laws in the heart of the man rather than the tables of stone. Jesus gave some comparison of the law of sin and death and the law of the Spirit. Here is what he said: "Ye have heard that it was said by them of old time, Thou shalt not kill; and whosoever shall kill shall be in danger of the judgment: But I say unto you, That whosoever is angry with his brother without a cause shall be in danger of the judgment" (Matt. 5:21). The law of sin and death said thou shall not kill, but the law of the Spirit puts in the heart of a man not to be angry with his brother, which may cause him to kill.

Then Jesus went on to say this: "Ye have heard that it was said by them of old time, Thou shalt not commit adultery: But I say unto you, That whosoever looketh on a woman to lust after her hath committed adultery with her already in his heart" (Matt. 5:27-28).

To summarize, the difference between the law of the Spirit and the law of sin and death is this: the Spirit places the law in the heart of man, and the law of sin and death places the law on stones, oftentimes never reaching the heart.

Let me share with you the plan that God has for us, the type of lifestyle required for us to receive his plan, and the type of lifestyle that will make void his promise. 1 John 3:1 states, "Behold, what manner of love the Father hath bestowed upon us, that we should be called the sons of God: therefore the world knoweth us not, because it knew him not." John is saying the world will not understand you if you serve God correctly.

John continues to say,

> *"Beloved, now are we the sons of God, and it doth not yet appear what we shall be: but we know that, when he shall appear, we shall be like him; for we shall see him as he is. And every man that hath*

this hope in him purified himself, even as he is pure. Whosoever committeth sin transgresseth also the law: for sin is the transgression of the law. And ye know that he was manifested to take away our sins; and in him is no sin. Whosoever abides in him sinneth not: whosoever sinneth hath not seen him, neither known him" (1 John 3:2-6).

He is saying that every man that has the hope of becoming his son must begin to purify himself (through the Word of God) even as He is pure.

1 John 3:7-8 states, "Little children, let no man deceive you: he that does righteousness is righteous, even as he is righteous. He that commits sin is of the devil, for the devil sinned from the beginning. For this purpose the Son of God was manifested, that he might destroy the works of the devil." John is telling you to not let any preacher deceive you. You are only righteous through submission to Jesus Christ, which will begin to change your heart to do what is right.

"Whosoever is born of God doth not commit sin; for his seed remains in him: and he cannot sin, because he is born of God. In this the children of God are manifest, and the children of the devil: whosoever doeth not righteousness is not of God, neither he that loveth not his brother" (1 John 3:9-10).

Peter stated in the book of Acts these words about himself, "And we are his witnesses of these things; and so is also the Holy

Ghost, whom God hath given to them that obey him" (Acts 5:32). You cannot receive the Spirit of God without a heart to obey God, and if anyone is training you how to speak in tongues, you are not receiving the Spirit of God like that. It came in like a mighty rushing wind, and it filled the whole house. The Holy Ghost will come to you when you make a conscious decision to completely follow him.

Jesus said, "If ye love me, keep my commandments. And I will pray the Father, and he shall give you another Comforter, that he may abide with you forever" (John 14:15-16). You cannot please God without it. No man is strong enough alone. We WERE all sinners. What changed my life is that God's Spirit came into me, changed my mind, and gave me a new way of thinking and living! The things I used to do, I didn't desire them anymore.

Jesus spoke these words to twelve common men, "Even the Spirit of truth; whom the world cannot receive, because it seeth him not, neither knoweth him: but ye know him; for he dwelleth with you, and shall be in you" (John 14:17). When Jesus said, "the world seeth him not," he really means the world did not recognize him as the Son of God nor understood all the things he spoke was of God. The reason why most people don't receive the true Spirit of God is that they don't understand its true purpose. Its purpose is for much more than to shout, dance, and speak in tongues. Tongues is a language that the Spirit of God will speak, but it has a far greater function than speaking in tongues. Have you ever observed anybody devil-possessed, bipolar, or with a split personality? There are spirits that cause these different personalities. Sometimes violent, sorrowful, and some even have strange body movements of torment and fear. Being filled with the Spirit of God will cause you to respond in a godly manner. You should experience stronger faith, courage, peace, and joy upon receiving God's Spirit. You need this!

If the Spirit of God be in you, Paul said, "for the law of the Spirit of life in Christ Jesus hath made me free from the law of sin and death" (Rom. 8:2). When you receive the Holy Ghost, it will free you from the law of sin and death.

Jesus said, "These things have I spoken unto you, being yet present with you. But the Comforter, which is the Holy Ghost, whom the Father will send in my name, he shall teach you all things, and bring all things to your remembrance, whatsoever I have said unto you" (John 14:25-26). The Spirit will start to teach you all things that are of God.

Jesus also stated this in another place about the function of the Spirit, "Howbeit when he, the Spirit of truth, is come, he will guide you into all truth: for he shall not speak of himself; but whatsoever he shall hear, that shall he speak: and he will shew you things to come" (John 16:13). The Spirit of truth will not come into a vessel that will not surrender to its leadership.

When you say "lord" to someone, that means they are your boss or your owner. For example, landlord means the owner of the property. Jesus stated, "Why call me Lord, Lord, and do not the things I say?" That means he is not your Lord if you do not obey him. So, we conclude that Jesus does not consider himself to be Lord over anyone that refuses to submit their lives to him. The Bible says, "Know ye not, that to whom ye yield yourselves servants to obey, his servants ye are to whom ye obey; whether of sin unto death, or of obedience unto righteousness?" (Rom. 6:16).

Examples of Often Misquoted Scriptures

I will begin to show you several other quotes that are misunderstood and exercised in the lives of people to their own destruction. Taking the Scriptures in error is equivalent to taking the wrong medicine prescribed for one thing and used for another. Incorrect use of medicine has been fatal to human beings! Likewise incorrect use of Scriptures can also be fatal to a Christian life and the goal of achieving eternal salvation.. God has said in Isaiah 55: 10-11, "For as the rain cometh down . . . and returneth not thither, but watereth the earth, and maketh it bring forth and bud, that it may give seed to the sower, and bread to the eater: So shall my word be that goeth forth out of my mouth: it shall not return unto me void, but it shall accomplish that which I please, and it shall prosper in the thing whereto I sent it." These Scriptures clearly show that with correct usage of God's Word we should experience the precise promises made by the Scriptures. Here are some examples of Scriptures spoken in error which have caused many not to believe God's Word; even some to die:

1) With his stripes, we are healed

2) We are all born in sin

3) Thou shall lend and not borrow

4) Thou shall be the head and not the tail

5) Thou shall be above and not beneath

6) The devil cometh not but to steal, kill, and destroy

7) Death and life are in the power of the tongue

I will show and explain these Scriptures and the error in which they are taught. Then, the correct meaning of these Scriptures will follow:

1) "With his stripes, we are healed." Believing this Scripture wrongfully suggests that Christians should be healed by the stripes of Jesus without the use of any other method. I have seen godly people die believing if they take medicine, visit a doctor, or use any other methods of healing, they were denying the faith in Jesus Christ's stripes. This erroneous teaching has caused death in many that had benign illnesses. But if attended to in a proper manner, it would have easily been corrected. "With his stripes we are healed" shows the fulfillment of the punishment Jesus took for our transgressions

and sin. Chastisement was a requirement by the law for human error. This is why God doesn't require us to be whipped anymore for the wrong we have done. Deut. 25:1-2 states, "If there be a controversy between men, and they come unto judgment, that the judges may judge them; then they shall justify the righteous and condemn the wicked. And it shall be, if the wicked man be worthy to be beaten, that the judge shall cause him to lie down, and to be beaten before his face, according to his fault, by a certain number." This Scripture truly explains Jesus himself taking the stripes for the bad behavior of believers, not at all stating that you should never become sick at any time. I have seen Christians refuse simple things such as x-rays, vitamins, blood transfusions, and vaccines, believing that they were immune from any sickness based on this Scripture, which is error.

The truth of the Scripture is that he was beaten for our transgressions, not at all suggesting that the stripes of Jesus Christ secure the healing of a sick person, but rather suggests that Jesus met the Law requirement for the whipping of a person that has done wrong. With his stripes we remain whole without taking stripes for the wrong we have done. This is not stating that Christians would not get sick. However, the Bible clearly explains that the prayer of faith shall save the sick. James 5:14-15 states, "Is any sick among you? Let him call for the elders of the church; and let them pray over him, anointing him with oil in the name of the Lord: And the prayer of faith shall save the sick, and the Lord shall raise him up; and if he have committed sins, they shall be forgiven him."

This passage in the Bible teaches us the importance of the elders of the church and prayer for the healing of the church. Christians should never believe that they are immune to the elements of this world, such as the common cold, viruses, diseases, and bacteria. The Christian's physical body is made no different than the sinner's. God has always instructed his people to care for their vessels with a balanced diet (Gen. 1:29) and proper rest (Exod. 20:8 states to remember the Sabbath day). Paul stated, "Bodily exercise profits little" (1 Tim. 4:8), so we see that with exercise, eating healthy, and with proper rest the Christian should remain healthy.

2) I use the term that is commonly used, "we are all born in sin" only because of the frequent use of this statement, but in truth, there is no Scripture that states we are all born in sin. I recognize this error has been taken from Psalm 51:5, where David states these words, but the meaning has been changed in modern teachings, "Behold, I was shapen in iniquity; and in sin did my mother conceive me." Nowhere is it written in the Bible that all men are born in sin.

The truth is David is explaining that his mom and dad were not married at the time of his conception. The baby is conceived in sin only when the mom and dad are not married. David's mother and father were not married to each other. For God said from the beginning, "be fruitful and multiply and replenish the earth." Heb. 13:4 clearly explains, "Marriage is honourable in all, and the bed undefiled: but whoremongers and adulterers God will judge." This Scripture outlines birth of children from married couples is undefiled. It's only defiled when childbirth comes by adultery and fornication. God would never command us to be fruitful and multiply if he was commanding us to commit sin. "Shapen in iniquity" means David's lifestyle was formed by the environment he was raised in and the lineage that preceded him. As an example, in David's lineage, Judah slept with his daughter-in-law, Tamar; Salmon, David's great grandfather, slept with Rahab, the harlot; David's grandfather Boaz, slept with Ruth a Moabite, and although they were married, it was forbidden by God; David himself was the product of an adulterous affair that he admits in Psalm 51:5.

Children that are raised in an environment of gangs, drugs, violence, and prostitution can say that the environment in which they were raised shaped their life. Those that are raised in environments of prejudice, racism, and hatred will have their lives shaped by the negative views and actions in these environments. Likewise, those individuals who raise their children in church and love will see the same behavior in their offspring.

In this Bible passage, David was pleading and explaining to God why he was engaged in such behavior. He was explaining to

God how he had acquired this behavior by his environment, not at all stating that all men were born in sin! If this had been the case, we would have seen in other Scriptures men being born in sin. Rom. 5:12-19 is another passage that men cite to support this error, but verse 12 states precisely what Paul was speaking about concerning an environment of sin: "Wherefore, as by one man sin entered in to the world, and death by sin; and so, death passed upon all men, for that all have sinned." Once again, this Scripture does not say that all men are born in sin. It simply says by one man sin came into the world, and death comes upon all men because all men have followed the pattern that has been set before them—sinning. This is like one child in the neighborhood bringing in drugs, and the whole neighborhood can become drug-infested. This does not say that all of the children were born addicts, just by one child introducing drugs, the whole neighborhood began to engage in drugs. This is what Paul is trying to convey to the church: Just like Adam introduced man to sin, and man willfully chose to follow a sinful lifestyle, Christ introduced to the world righteousness and obedience to God, and through this introduction of righteousness, man may choose obedience unto God. If these Scriptures are used to say that all men were made sinners by Adam's sin, which has nothing to do with their choice of lifestyle, then it's also saying that ALL MEN are righteous having nothing to do with their lifestyle. That would mean serial killers, rapists, terrorists, pedophiles, robbers, Satan worshippers, and any other evil would be righteous, simply because one man, Jesus Christ, was righteous. Rom. 5:18-19 is the Scripture that is used to support this error, "Therefore as by the offence of one judgment came upon all men to condemnation; even so by the righteousness of one the free gift came upon all men unto justification of life. For as by one man's disobedience many were made sinners, so by the obedience of one shall many be made righteous." Verse 19 states that many shall be made righteous, NOT ALL MEN are born in sin, but many shall be made righteous. Not those that call him Lord only, but those that do the things he says according to Luke 7:46, which states, "And why call ye me, Lord, Lord and do not the things which I say?" Matt. 7:21 also confirms this statement, "Not every one that saith unto me, Lord, Lord, shall enter into the kingdom of heaven; but he that doeth the will of my Father which is in heaven." Through these teachings of Jesus, he caused many to be made righteous by turning them from their sinful lifestyle.

Statements 3), 4), and 5), "thou shall lend and not borrow, thou shall be the head and not the tail, and thou shall be above and not beneath," These Scriptures are true when they are accompanied with obedience to all of God's Word according to Deut. 28. To expect these things without teaching obedience to God is error.

6) Here is another frequent error in nearly all of the churches

today: "the devil cometh not but to steal, kill and destroy." Once again, I used a commonly quoted statement; however, this statement is not in the Bible anywhere. Let me take the time to explain the source of this frequently quoted error. In John 10:10, Jesus stated, "The thief cometh not, but for to steal, and kill, and destroy: I am come that they might have life and that they might have it more abundantly." The Scripture stated that the "thief" comes to steal, kill, and destroy. Jesus is speaking in terms of a true shepherd that approaches the sheep and a false shepherd that comes to the sheep. The true shepherd comes to feed, lead, heal, and protect the sheep and sometimes loses his life to protect the sheep from wolves and other wild beasts. The false shepherd comes to the same sheep that belong to another with the intent to deceive and destroy the sheep for his own gain. In John 10:12, the thief that approaches for monetary purpose will never give his life for the sake of the sheep, but rather steal and literally kill the sheep for his own purpose. This error is very dangerous to the entire Christian community because they have been given a delusion of the devil being the thief, whereas the truth is this Scripture is talking about preachers coming to the sheep for their own gain. Through many gimmicks they have stolen, killed, and destroyed the finances, faith, and morale of believers. This error has caused the Christians to not recognize the preacher's intent, while they promise the people great rewards. The thief (the preacher) takes their money, and many times, this leads to the ruin of uncertain and confused Christians. This is the good side: Jesus also said in John 10:8 speaking of preachers, "All that ever came before me are thieves and robbers: but the sheep did not hear them." Jesus is explaining in this passage that the sheep, which submit to Jesus's voice, will not follow the voice of another preacher that is not parallel with his voice. In simple terms, they should teach entirely and only the things that Jesus taught.

There is no Scripture throughout the entire Bible stating that the devil has stolen anything from one person. This error of the devil coming to steal, kill, and destroy has made its way into many of our songs, sermons, testimonies, and spiritual warfare. As we fight to regain spiritual and natural material believed to be stolen by the devil, the true thief stays at large. Now, the Bible describes the devil or Satan as one that tempts, entices, accuses, oppresses, and deceives. There is no record in the Bible of the devil killing or stealing anything. When you have lost something spiritually, it was not because of any theft on Satan's part. The truth of the matter is you sold it for pleasure and fleshly sensations that he tempted or enticed you to do. James 1:14 states, "Every man is tempted, when he is drawn away of his own lust, and enticed."

Satan's warfare against believers is to present to them things that they desire and entice them with it. He knows our struggles as humans, so he presents things to us in order to cause us to willfully leave our shepherd (Jesus) for pleasure. This is not through theft or murder but enticement. This error is so damaging because it prevents you from identifying the true reasons for your loss. For example, when you arrest the wrong person for the crime, the criminal is still allowed to roam freely. I must note, I have nothing good to say about the devil, but arresting the devil for a crime that is committed by false preachers will never stop the crime until the thieves and murderers are identified. The murderer and thief continue to steal, kill, and destroy because they are not detected.

Now, I will clearly disclose who the real criminals are and the methods they use to deceive. Jesus warned, "Beware of false prophets, which come to you in sheep's clothing, but inwardly they are ravening wolves" (Matt. 7:15). Jesus explains the ones that are most detrimental to our souls, spiritual lives, and financial estates are those that we trust the most to lead, feed, and protect us. God often warned about these false shepherds in the Old Testament. Isa. 56:10-11 states, "His watchmen are blind: they are all ignorant, they are all dumb dogs, they cannot bark; sleeping, lying down, loving to slumber. Yea, they are greedy dogs which can never have enough, and they are shepherds that cannot understand: they all look to their own way, every one for his gain, from his quarter." This Scripture explains the shepherds are preachers that are in the midst of us whose primary purpose is for their own gain. The gospel of John 10:1-10 is where this error is taken from. Jesus explained the method and the motive of false shepherds as they approach a flock of sheep that belong to another shepherd (Jesus). They appear to be true shepherds, hoping to deceive the sheep as if they had the sheep's interest at heart. But the intent of these wolves, appearing to be shepherds of concern, is to steal, kill, and eat the sheep.

The true sheep know the intent of a false shepherd when he approaches and will not respond to their gimmicks and tricks. Jesus explains throughout John 10 that his sheep know his voice and a stranger they will not follow. These Scriptures explain how true sheep of God trust in God's methods for prosperity, health, and deliverance. The false shepherds offer alternative methods without faith and commitment to God's Word, but these are the things that God instructs his people to do to prosper in all things—repentance, prayer, obedience, and faith are essential. Through alternative methods (not from the words of Jesus) false shepherds guarantee all things. Jesus stated he is the way the truth and the life, therefore, any method that is taught to the sheep that has not come from the mouth of Christ is described by Jesus as a method of a thief.

Let us look into some of these methods that are contrary to the instructions that come from Christ. The true shepherd understands that freely he has received and freely he should give. The

Bible gives no advantage for praying with a cloth on your head or buying a special Bible, using a certain oil, blowing a particular horn, or any other mundane material. The true shepherd will emphasize that the salvation of God is free, and according to Acts 8:20, the gift of God cannot be purchased with money.

It is by faith, prayer, and repentance that God freely gives us all things. James 1:5 states, "If any of you lack wisdom, let him ask of God, that giveth to all men liberally, and upbraideth not; and it shall be given him." James continues to say that you must ask in faith, not wavering for a double-minded man shall not receive anything of the Lord. I would like to note, instead of teaching you the need for prayer, repentance, and faith towards God, these thieves and murderers teach all these things are received through your money. They will put more value on your contribution and sowing a seed to them. Jesus taught, "Seek ye first the kingdom of God, and his righteousness; and all these things shall be added unto you" (Matt. 6:33). What grieves me so much about these thieves is that they brag about how much money they have and property they own without debt, which was supposedly gained by their contributions to others. Through this message they literally steal, kill, and destroy the welfare of the poor by promising them that if they give more, all their needs will be met.

In my early ministry, I saw one evangelist after another that

I invited to come to our church, with these schemes, and after they left, I had to pay utility bills and buy food for so many people that allowed these thieves to trick them to borrow money, give their savings, and to pledge what they did not have. I would like to say, I believe in cheerful giving more than they all because the Bible says in 2 Cor. 9:7, "Every man according as he purposeth in his heart so let him give; not GRUDGINGLY, or of NECESSITY: for God loveth a cheerful giver." No person should feel that blessings are determined only upon the amount of money they give.

As we read Jesus's sermon upon the mountain, he stated the blessing plans, and he said nothing about the amount of money that was given to determine your blessings. These are the words he spoke in Matt. 5:1-11: Blessed are the pure in heart, blessed are the meek, blessed are they which do hunger and thirst after righteousness, blessed are the merciful, blessed are the pure in heart, blessed are the peacemakers, blessed are they that are persecuted for righteousness sake. A godly minister will teach the sheep of God that these are the things that determine their blessings. These wolves will never emphasize the importance of these Scriptures in receiving your blessings from God. Instead, they will make light of these Scriptures that clearly explain how to obtain your blessings. Through the process of teaching another way of success, they STEAL the sheep of Christ to follow their own theology, ideology, dreams, visions, and prophecies. Through these deceptive methods the sheep no longer recognize their original shepherd's voice (Jesus).

I have gone to many places over forty years of ministry and have been so disheartened to see "Christ's sheep" ignore his word when it is spoken. This describes precisely what Jesus meant when he said the thief comes to STEAL, KILL, and DESTROY. When the sheep can no longer determine the voice or words of the true shepherd (Jesus), who lays down his life for them, they have been stolen from their original shepherd. The voice of their original shepherd they fail to recognize. The sheep are now trusting in a denomination, a preacher, or teacher that ignores some of the teachings of Jesus. Jer. 23:1 states, "Woe unto the pastors that DESTROY and scatter the sheep of my pasture! saith the Lord." Also, in Ezek. 34:2-5, God tells the prophet Ezekiel to prophesy against the shepherds of Israel that feed themselves and not the flock. He tells them they eat the fat of the sheep; they clothe themselves with the wool and KILL them that are fed.

I would like to note that throughout the entire Bible, God often warns of the greatest enemy (excluding Satan) to the true church are false prophets, false teachers, false pastors, and false doctrine. In 1 John 2:18-19, it says,

> *"Little children, it is the last time: and as ye have heard that antichrist shall come, even now are*

there many antichrists; whereby we know that it is the last time. They went out from us, but they were not of us; for if they had been of us, they would no doubt have continued with us: but they went out, that they might be made manifest that they were not all of us."

The apostle John explains in this text that the antichrists are many and went out from among the church. While the church is looking for and avoiding the Beast and the number 666, they have opened up their hearts to accept another antichrist. Jesus stated in Luke 11:23, "He that is not with me is against me: and he that gathereth not with me scattereth."

The true shepherd or prophet will gather the people to all the teachings of Jesus and not to any other doctrine which Paul describes in 2 Cor. 11:2-4, (emphasis mine)

> *"For I am jealous over you with godly jealousy: for I have espoused you to one husband, that I may present you as a chaste virgin to Christ. But I fear, lest by any means, as the serpent beguiled Eve through his subtilty, so your minds should be corrupted from the simplicity that is in Christ. For if he that cometh preacheth another Jesus, whom we have not preached, or if ye receive another spirit, which ye have not received, or another gospel, which ye have not accepted, ye might well BEAR WITH HIM."*

Paul is instructing that if we at any time receive teachings that vary from the teachings of Jesus Christ, the true shepherd, we are annulling the marriage or engagement with Christ and entering into a relationship with a different shepherd (other than Jesus). Paul states we must BEAR WITH HIM; that is to say that Christ is relinquishing all liabilities for you and your soul, and now you should rely on the new teacher, preacher, denomination, or theology to deliver, save and protect you.

Jesus stated, "I am the way, the truth, and the life: no man cometh unto the Father, but by me" (John 14:6). For example, when a man and a woman are engaged for marriage, and the woman begins to date another man while she is engaged, this produces jealousy and anger, which ultimately leads to separation. Paul is warning of this break-up between Christ and his church, simply by mixing man's ideas or theology, denominational teachings, and made-up religious holidays with Jesus Christ's teachings. Also, to ignore the things Jesus commanded us will likewise destroy the relationship. For example, these are often ignored commandments given by Jesus Christ, ignored by the church: Be ye therefore perfect even as your Father in heaven is perfect (Matt. 5:48); Except you repent you shall all likewise perish (Luke 13:3); Not every one that saith unto me Lord, Lord shall enter into the kingdom of heaven but he that does the will of my Father which is in heaven (Matt. 7:21); If we will not forgive every man their trespass your Father in heaven will not forgive you (Matt. 18:35); Love your enemy, bless them that curse you, do good to them that hate you and pray for them that despitefully misuse you (Matt. 5:44). By leaving off these critical points of salvation, the THIEF has led you away from continuing a connection with the words of Jesus only.

I must say, a true preacher will see eye to eye with Christ, and only Jesus's words will they speak. The Bible says, "Thy watchmen shall lift up the voice; with the voice together shall they sing: for they shall see eye to eye, when the Lord shall bring again Zion" (Isa. 52:8). The true question is, have you been stolen or led away by a false shepherd's voice that sounds similar to the genuine shepherd? I will give you a small quiz so that you may examine yourself to see what shepherd you are following. Circle the answer of your choice. Here we go.

1. There was only one perfect man. True or False

2. By grace, we are allowed to continue sinning in the New Testament. True or False

3. Once saved, always saved. True or False

4. We are all sinners saved by grace. True or False

5. Confessing Christ makes you right regardless of how you live. True or False

You should have answered "False" for all of these statements. Give me a moment to express by Scripture the truth, according to the Bible on these teachings.

[1. There was only one perfect man. False.] The Bible lists Job as a perfect man in chapter 1. In Job 1:8, God testifies again that Job was perfect. Gen. 6:9 states, " . . . Noah was a just man and perfect in his generations, and Noah walked with God." Also, Ps. 37:37 states, "Mark the perfect man, and behold the upright: for the end of that man is peace." The Bible will never tell you to mark or mimic a perfect man if there was no one perfect to mark. Jesus said in Matthew 5:48, "Be ye therefore perfect, even as your Father which is in heaven is perfect." God says to Abraham in Gen. 17:1, " . . . Walk before me, and be thou perfect." In Heb. 6:1, ". . . Let us go on unto perfection; not laying again the foundation of repentance from dead works, and of faith toward God." God would not command us to be perfect if this was an impossible task. I have given you Bible Scriptures that clearly show God's request for his people. The question you should ask yourself: "Whom do I believe in? The words of Jesus, or statements of ministers, which say, 'No one is perfect.'" Please examine what you truly believe.

[2. By grace, we are allowed to continue sinning in the New Testament. False.] The true answer for number two is Titus 2:11-12 which states, "For the grace of God that bringeth salvation hath appeared to all men, teaching us that, denying ungodliness and worldly lust, we should live soberly, righteously, and godly, IN THIS PRESENT WORLD." The question is asked and answered correctly in

Rom. 6:1-2, ". . . Shall we continue in sin, that grace may abound? God forbid. How shall we, that are dead to sin, live any longer therein?" The phrase "God forbid" means never shall it be. Grace will never abound in the life of a person that continues to sin. I would like to make note of a Scripture that is often used to suggest that all men are sinners. This is perhaps one of the most misunderstood Scriptures in the Bible. 1 John 1:8-9 says, "If we say that we have no sin, we deceive ourselves, and the truth is not in us. If we confess our sins, he is faithful and just to forgive us our sins, and to cleanse us from all unrighteousness." Reading this in the true narrative of the epistle of John explains that all men have sinned and are sinners without confessing their sins and allowing the faithfulness of Jesus to forgive us and clean us from all our sins. It is not stating that once Jesus cleans you from your sin you remain a sinner. When Jesus cleans you from your sin you are completely cleansed from sin. You should now be able to walk in a new way of living. The very next Scripture in 1 John 2:1 states, "My little children, these things write I unto you, that ye SIN NOT. And if any man sin, we have an advocate with the Father, Jesus Christ the righteous." John stated IF any man sin, we have an advocate with the Father. That is IF any should sin, Christ is merciful to forgive us of our sins when we repent; not at all suggesting that we would continue to sin. 1 John 2:3-4 says, "And hereby we do know that we know him, if we keep his commandments. He that saith, I know him, and keepth not his commandments, is a liar, and the truth is not in him." John continues in 1 John 3:6-8, "Whosoever abideth in him sinneth not: whosoever sinneth hath not seen him, neither known him. Little children, let no man deceive you: he that doeth righteousness is righteous, even as he is righteous."

[3. Once saved, always saved. False.] Let me show you where this error has derived from, then I may answer the question correctly. In Heb. 5:8-9, "Though he were a Son, yet learned he obedience by the things which he suffered; and being made perfect, he became the author of <u>eternal salvation</u> unto all them that <u>obey him</u>." This Scripture points out clearly, that eternal salvation is given to all those that are obedient to him. Paul stated in 1 Cor. 9:27, "But I keep under my body, and bring it into subjection: lest that by any means, when I have preached to others, I myself should be a castaway." Paul is expressing in this writing the importance of maintaining control over his life to prevent Christ from casting him away. Some suppose Heb. 13:5-6 confirms "once saved, always saved," but the truth of this Scripture explains God's loyalty and commitment to always be a helper and provider for the needs of his people. The Scripture states, "Let your conversation be without covetousness; and be content with such things as ye have: for he hath said, I will never leave thee, nor forsake thee. So that we may boldly say, The Lord is my helper, and I will not fear what man shall do unto me." The truth is [He will never leave you nor forsake you] God will never ignore your physical and spiritual needs. It is error to believe that with a corrupt lifestyle you can maintain a good status with God. For the Scripture states in Isa. 59:2, "But your iniquities have separated between you and your God, and your sins have hid his face from you, that he will not hear."

Last of all, Peter describes the converted Christian that goes back to a sinful lifestyle being in a worse condition with God than someone never converted.

> *"For if after they have escaped the pollutions of the world through the knowledge of the Lord and Saviour Jesus Christ, they are again entangled therein, and overcome, the latter end is worse with them than the beginning. For it had been better for them not to have known the way of righteousness, than, after they have known it, to turn from the holy commandment delivered unto them" (2 Pet. 2:20-21).*

Paul also stated in Rom. 2:6, "[God] will render to every man according to his deeds." Jesus said he that endures until the end the same shall be saved. We must continue to do what is right to be saved. When the Christian errs or sins, they must repent to be saved. They cannot continue to do wrong without repentance and expect to be saved. The Bible says that whosoever covers his sin shall not prosper, but whoever confesses them and forsakes them shall have mercy. So, we see there must be a resistance to sin to obtain mercy.

[4. We are all sinners saved by grace. False.] There is no Scripture that states we are all sinners saved by grace. Let me show you where these errors derived from. "For all have sinned and come short of the glory of God" Rom. 3:23. This Scripture explains that all "have," past tense, not all "are," present tense. 1 John 1:8 reads, "If we say that we have no sin, we deceive ourselves, and the truth is not in us." This Scripture was intended to show precisely that all men that have not confessed their sins to God still have sin in their lives. It was not to say that with confession and repentance sin is still attached to us as it is so believed today. The very next verse states, "If we confess our sins, he is faithful and just to forgive us our sins, and to cleanse us from all unrighteousness" (1 John 1: 9). Once one is cleansed from sin, he has no sin on him anymore because he has been cleaned. If the statement is true that sin is always on us, then we are never clean at any time. This thought contradicts Jesus's words, "Now ye are clean through the word which I have spoken unto you" (John 15:3). It also contradicts 1 John 2:1, "My little children, these things write I unto you, that ye sin not. And if any man sin, we have an advocate with the Father, Jesus Christ the righteous." Here he is saying we should begin a new life of resistance to sin; he also explains that if we sin, we should not give up because we have an advocate with the Father who is Jesus Christ the righteous, for he offered himself a sacrifice for our sins. Using Scripture out of its context will always create error in the Christian church.

[5. Confessing Christ makes you right regardless of how you live. False.] This answer is clear according to the words of Jesus Christ when he spoke these words in Luke 6:46, "And why call ye me, Lord, Lord and do not the things which I say?" Being much more direct concerning this, he stated these words,

> *"Not every one that saith unto me, Lord, Lord, shall enter into the kingdom of heaven; but he that doeth the will of my Father which is in heaven. Many will say to me in that day, Lord, Lord, have we not prophesied in thy name? And in thy name have cast out devils? And in thy name done many wonderful works? And then will I profess unto them, I never knew you: depart from me, ye that work iniquity"* (Matt. 7:21-23).

I often cry and weep for so many people who devote their whole lives to working in ministry and prophesying but not taking to heart to do his will. When they face him in the last day, they will be told to depart from him although they called him Lord and confessed him as Lord. If Jesus is your Lord, you will do what he said.

As I pointed out many false statements in this chapter that people believe in, we must conclude that a counterfeit dollar will not hold up at a bank, or a fake ticket will not get you into a sporting activity. When we attempt to spend counterfeit money, we fall into the category of fraud, and so is it with false doctrine and teachings. It is each individual's responsibility to examine the things that they trust and believe in to be sure they are true according to God's Word.

CHAPTER 2

How the Spirit Speaks to the Church

The book of Revelation should not be considered a scary book, as many people believe it to be. Instead, let us recognize the word *revelation* means revealing, something revealed, or something that needs to be revealed to the church. The book was given to the church to reveal their status with God and their need to repent to avoid future judgment for lack of repentance, which they knew not. John was to write unto every church how God viewed their behavior and what to expect in the end if there was no repentance. This also gave comfort to the church that endured grief to be obedient to God. Only two out of seven churches did God commend their lifestyle as being acceptable. There were five churches that God revealed to them in this book their need to repent.

In the book of Revelation, you will see Scriptures like the following: "He that hath an ear let him hear what the Spirit saith unto the churches" (Rev. 2:7). When you read these Scriptures, do you ever stop to ask, "Am I hearing what the Spirit says unto the church?"

In this chapter, I will show you:

1) How the Spirit speaks to the church

2) How to discern the Spirit speaking versus man's thoughts

3) When a doctrine or someone's teaching is coming from man's ideology, theology, or philosophy.

Apostle Peter stated, "For we have not followed cunningly devised fables, when we made known unto you the power and coming of our Lord Jesus Christ, but were eyewitnesses of his majesty" (2 Pet. 1:16). In this Scripture, Peter is saying that the early church leaders did not follow their own thoughts or ideas, and neither did they teach cunningly created or devised fables that were made up. In 2 Pet. 1:17-18, Peter added, "For he received from God the Father honour and glory, when there came such a voice to him from the excellent glory, This is my beloved Son, in whom I am well pleased. And this voice which came from heaven we heard, when we were with him in the holy mount."

It certainly sounds very convincing to hear a voice from heaven say anything, and it was certainly convincing to hear the voice say, "This is my beloved Son, in whom I am well pleased." But Peter did not stop here. He went on to add in verse 19, "We have also a more sure word of prophecy; whereunto ye do well that ye take heed, as unto a light that shineth in a dark place, until the day dawn, and the day star arise in your hearts:" Peter classified the voice that came out of heaven as prophecy but went on to say that we have something that is more sure or trustworthy than the voice that came from heaven (he was speaking about the Old Testament Scriptures).

He went on to say, "Knowing this first, that no prophecy of the scripture is of any private interpretation" (2 Pet. 1:20). Peter classified the voice from heaven as prophecy, here he is classifying the Scriptures as prophecy. But he adds, ". . . no prophecy of the scripture is of any private interpretation." The interpretation of Scripture should not come from man's ideology.

Peter makes this point even more clearly in verse 21, "For the prophecy came not in old time by the will of man: but holy men of God spake as they were moved by the Holy Ghost." When holy men spoke the Old Testament Scriptures, they were moved by the Holy Ghost. They did not speak their own thoughts, ideologies, or theories. They were moved by the Holy Ghost whenever they prophesied or spoke God's Word.

So according to Peter, when you hear what the Spirit is saying unto the church, you are hearing what the Scriptures have stated. You also know that the prophecy from the Scriptures of old did not come by the will of men, but it came by men as the Spirit of God moved them. Are you basing your life on a prophecy that someone has spoken to you, and not considering what the Scripture states concerning you? We should not take heed to any prophecy that does not parallel with the Scriptures. For example, someone may prophesy to you saying, "Thus said the Lord, you are blessed abundantly." This is only true when the Scriptures state the same concerning you. Matt. 5:1-11 states, the pure in heart, the peacemakers, the merciful, the meek, those that mourn, and those that are hungry for righteousness are blessed.

Peter warns us to be cautious of modern prophecies, stating,

> *"But there were false prophets also among the people, even as there shall be false teachers among you, who privily shall bring in damnable heresies, even denying the Lord that bought them, and bring upon themselves swift destruction. And many shall follow their pernicious ways; by reason of whom the way of truth shall be evil spoken of" (2 Pet. 2:1-2).*

As Peter reminds us, many church people with an intent or desire to be saved will follow the pernicious (or wicked) way of a prophet that prophesies or preaches a lie to them by misusing a Scripture in a wrong way. Peter is saying that there will be more people clinging to the lies of the false prophet than to what God has said because they don't know how to determine when God is speaking, and how to examine a minister when he preaches.

Paul gives us some insight into this as well from Acts 17:2, "And Paul, as his manner was, went in unto them, and three sabbath days reasoned with them out of the Scriptures." When Paul reasoned with them, he preached out of the Scriptures. Now we should note that Paul did not begin his ministry until seventeen years after Christ was crucified. None of Paul's teachings were derived from the New Testament Bible because it had not yet been written. From the source of the Old Testament writings, Paul wrote and taught the New Testament, which we now are under. These are the epistles written by Paul: Romans, 1 and 2 Corinthians, Galatians, Ephesians, Philippians, Colossians, 1 and 2 Thessalonians, 1 and 2 Timothy, Titus, and Philemon. The source of all these books that Paul wrote was the Old Testament. He wrote unto those churches epistles, which are letters. However, he used Scriptures in his letters, but he wrote letters like I am writing to you, and they were classified as epistles. To be precise we must continue to classify the Old Testament as the Scriptures, and Paul's writings as New Testament epistles.

Just like Paul, I use Scriptures in my teachings. But you should not grab my teachings and say, "These are the Scriptures." You may hear my tape, and if it's written down, you can say this is Apostle Wendell Archie's epistle, his writing or his book. Although my book is composed from the Scriptures, it should never be called the Scriptures.

Peter makes this point clear in 2 Pet. 3:15-16,

> *"And account that the longsuffering of our*
> *Lord is salvation; even as our beloved brother Paul*

also according to the wisdom given unto him hath written unto you; As also in all his epistles, speaking in them of these things; in which are some things hard to be understood, which they that are unlearned and unstable wrest, as they do also the other scriptures, unto their own destruction."

Peter classified Paul's writings as epistles, not Scriptures.

So, as you see in verse 16, Peter did not say "in all Paul's scriptures," he said, "in all Paul's epistles." Paul noted that when people did not understand his teachings because they were unlearned in the Scriptures of old, they did not recognize the source of Paul's writings. Since they did not recognize where Paul's message came from, they would take his teaching and corrupt the whole church. Remember, the ones who made these blunders were those who were unstable in the Scriptures. But those who understood Paul's teachings were those who also knew the Scriptures.

Jesus also showed the necessity of knowing the Scriptures: "Search the scriptures; for in them ye think ye have eternal life: and they are they which testify of me" (John 5:39). Jesus was not talking about the New Testament. The Scriptures were written on scrolls. As holy men spoke, scribes were writing down what they were saying. Their words were written on calfskin, pasted together, and rolled up to form a book, such as the books of Isaiah and Jeremiah.

Keep in mind that all of Paul's teachings were derived from

Scriptures, and everything he taught came from what was written of old. When you do not know what was written of old, you cannot determine truth from error when a Scripture is misquoted. You can't understand Paul if you have no clue where it came from; you will be confused. Unfortunately, that is how the church is today, confused.

I encourage everyone to purchase a reference Bible. By doing so, when you read where Paul says, "it is written," you can go back in the Old Testament and see where he got his words. Similarly, when you see him say, "The Lord said," you can find it written in the Old Testament.

Churches are being tricked because they don't study their Bibles anymore, and they are unstable in serving God! Instead, they take heed to the man who abuses or misuses the Scriptures! Many delight in the minister that makes them feel better because they enjoy what is being said; they accept it as truth. What you believe and receive can hurt you if it's not truth.

Just remember, every time Paul preached, he used the Scriptures. Those who heard and wanted to understand went back to the source of Paul's messages. Acts 17:2, 11, states, "And Paul, as his manner was, went in unto them, and three sabbath days reasoned with them out of the scriptures . . . These were more noble than those in Thessalonica, in that they received the word with all readiness of mind, and searched the scriptures daily, whether those things were so." These men were noble enough to search the Scriptures daily. When they heard Paul preach something, they went home and searched to see whether it was so. That's how they knew if Paul was telling the truth or not.

Paul preached Christ out of the Scriptures. Acts 17:3, "Opening and alleging, that Christ must needs have suffered, and risen again from the dead; and that this Jesus, whom I preach unto you, is Christ." Here, it is clear that Paul preached about Jesus Christ out of the Scriptures. Jesus is not just in the New Testament, but he is also in the Old Testament.

In the book of Revelation, Jesus spoke unto the church of Sardis that believed in him and had been baptized, that they were dead! Jesus went on to say to another church in Revelation,

> "Notwithstanding I have a few things against thee, because thou sufferest that woman Jezebel, which calleth herself a prophetess, to teach and to seduce my servants to commit fornication, and to eat things sacrificed unto idols. And I gave her space to repent of her fornication; and she repented not. Behold, I will cast her into a bed, and them that commit adultery with her into great tribulation, except they repent of their deeds. And I will kill her children with death; and all the churches shall know that I am he which searcheth the reins and hearts: and I will give unto every one of you according to your works" (Rev. 2:20-23).

Many believe that if you are in church, you are all right. The preachers today promise everybody life, just like the serpent promised life to Eve. Paul warned Timothy about letting down his guard saying these words, "But continue thou in the things which thou hast learned and hast been assured of, knowing of whom thou hast learned them" (2 Tim. 3:14). Specifically, Paul was letting Timothy know how the church would change. He told Timothy that deceivers would come, and men would be lovers of themselves, instead of lovers of God. Paul tells his young minister (Timothy was a preacher) not to get caught in the ways that preachers are going. Instead, he should continue in the things that he had learned from Paul.

Paul also referred Timothy back to the Scriptures for guidance. He stated in 2 Tim. 3:15, "And that from a child thou hast known the holy scriptures, which are able to make thee wise unto salvation through faith which is in Christ Jesus." He told Timothy that from a child, he had been taught the Scriptures, and those Scriptures were able to make him wise. So, you should not rely on the preacher, other interpretations of theology, or religious beliefs not supported by scripture.

Paul reinforced his message to Timothy. Specifically, he added in 2 Tim. 3:16, "All scripture is given by inspiration of God, and is profitable for doctrine, for reproof, for correction, for instruction in righteousness . . ." Again, he is not talking about epistles but Scriptures. I've seen Paul say in epistles, "I have no commandment of the Lord but I give my own judgment." Scriptures do not give their own judgment. By way of further example, in another epistle, Paul said in 1 Cor. 5:9, "I wrote unto you in an epistle not to company with fornicators," but he wrote another epistle to change that statement. In 1 Cor. 5:11, he said, "But now I have written unto you not to keep company, if any man that is called a brother be a fornicator, or covetous, or an idolater, or a railer, or a drunkard, or an extortioner; with such an one no not to eat." Again, Scriptures do not alter and change because they were not given by the ideology of men. Many times, Paul said, "in my opinion," but Scriptures do not give opinions. None of the Scriptures are opinionated.

So, is Paul teaching accurately? Yes, he is. The Scriptures should be used for reproof. With the Scriptures, you can reprove or correct someone. You can correct someone if they go contrary to the Scriptures, and instruct them in righteousness.

Paul also addressed situations when some do not believe or have faith in the word. He stated in Rom. 3:3-4, "For what if some did not believe? Shall their unbelief make the faith of God without effect? God forbid: yea, let God be true, but every man a liar; as it is written, that thou mightest be justified in thy sayings, and mightest overcome when thou art judged." Here, Paul is saying to let God be true and every man a liar, that you might be justified in what you say. Then you will overcome when you are judged on what you do or say.

Now how was Paul so confident in what he said? It is because he was using Scripture. Here is another error most churches have of Paul's teachings in Rom. 3:10-12, "As it is written, there is none righteous, no, not one: There is none that understandeth, there is none that seeketh after God. They are all gone out of the way, they are together become unprofitable; there is none that doeth good, no, not one." When he says, "As it is written," he is talking about the Old Testament. Today preachers lie and say that there is none good in the church. They have misunderstood the passage. Paul quoted Psalm 14:1-3 when he wrote Rom. 3:10. Psalm 14:1-3 states, "The fool hath said in his heart, There is no God. They are corrupt, they have done abominable works, there is none that doeth good. The LORD looked down from heaven upon the children of men, to see if there were any that did understand, and seek God. They are all gone aside, they are all together become filthy: there is none that doeth good, no, not one." Here Paul is clearly talking about the fool that hath said in his heart, there is no God. There is none of these that are good.

Put more clearly, Paul is saying that you are a fool if you believe that there is no God. Second, Paul is saying that no man who does not believe in God is good. Put another way, there is not one person who does not believe in God who will repent. But I'm not going to say that there is no holy preacher or holy person. It's the fool who does not believe in God; every one of them would do evil.

Here is another misunderstood Scripture: Romans 8:35-36, "Who shall separate us from the love of Christ? Shall tribulation, or distress, or persecution, or famine, or nakedness, or peril, or sword?" Many preachers use this passage to teach that even if we sin, nothing can separate us from the love of God. This is error. Instead, this verse is saying that you should not let anything separate you from the love of God. For example, just because someone did not allow you to preach, you want to separate from the body. You have allowed this to separate you from the love of God. Rom. 8:36 states,

> *"As it is written, For thy sake we are killed all the day long; we are accounted as sheep for the slaughter."*

> And here in the Old Testament, Psalm 44:17-22 states, *"All this is come upon us; yet have we not forgotten thee, neither have we dealt falsely in thy covenant. Our heart is not turned back, neither have our steps declined from thy way; Though thou hast sore broken us in the place of dragons, and covered us with the shadow of death. If we have forgotten the name of our God, or stretched out our hands to a strange god; Shall not God search this out? For he knoweth the secrets of the heart. Yea, for thy sake are we killed all the day long; we are counted as sheep for the slaughter."*

Above, the psalmist is talking about tribulation they endured for God's sake. He stated that we are killed all the day long and said we have not gone back from your commandments. Many preachers teach that we can sin, but still will not be separated from the love of God. But Paul is saying we have kept God's commandments although tribulation came, which is the correct reading of the verse as supported by the Scripture.

Another regularly misunderstood verse is Romans 9:13, "As it is written, Jacob have I loved, but Esau have I hated." Here, Paul is saying that God said he hated one but loved the other. Again, he got this verse from the Old Testament. But you will say that God loves the world! Yes, he does, but that does not mean he loves every personality.

Paul's source is found in Mal. 1:2-4.

> *"I have loved you, saith the LORD. Yet ye say, Wherein hast thou loved us? Was not Esau Jacob's brother? saith the LORD: yet I loved Jacob, And I hated Esau, and laid his mountains and his heritage waste for the dragons of the wilderness. Whereas Edom saith, We are impoverished, but we will return and build the desolate places; thus saith the LORD of hosts, They shall build, but I will throw down; and they shall call them, The border of wickedness, and, The people against whom the LORD hath indignation for ever."*

This is an example of someone attempting to build for God but not pleasing God. For example, if someone breaks into your house and brings you a gift from some of the merchandise they stole from you, would you be pleased with that gift? Without getting your life straight with God your building is in vain.

Here's another example of Paul using Scripture in his epistles: Rom. 10:5, "For Moses describeth the righteousness which is of the Law, that the man which doeth those things shall live by them." Paul understood by reading the Law, Moses gave a description of how to be right according to the Law. So, when Paul makes a statement quoting Moses or any other prophet, you should be able to find the original quotation of that prophet in the Old Testament.

In this regard, he went further to state the following in Rom. 10:6-8,

> "But the righteousness which is of faith speaketh on this wise, Say not in thine heart, Who shall ascend into heaven? (that is, to bring Christ down from above:) Or, Who shall descend into the deep? (that is, to bring up Christ again from the dead.) But what saith it? The word is nigh thee, even in thy mouth, and in thy heart: that is, the word of faith, which we preach."

Again, you are supposed to be able to go back and find what Paul means by examining the original context in the Old Testament. This passage was taken from Deut. 30:10-14.

> "If thou shalt hearken unto the voice of the LORD thy God, to keep his commandments and his statutes which are written in this book of the law, and

if thou turn unto the LORD thy God with all thine heart, and with all thy soul. For this commandment which I command thee this day, it is not hidden from thee, neither is it far off. It is not in heaven, that thou shouldest say, Who shall go up for us to heaven, and bring it unto us, that we may hear it, and do it? Neither is it beyond the sea, that thou shouldest say, Who shall go over the sea for us, and bring it unto us, that we may hear it, and do it? But the word is very nigh unto thee, in thy mouth, and in thy heart, that thou mayest do it."

It is clear from reading the Scripture that Paul is saying that the confession that you make with your mouth of the Lord Jesus has to be in your heart for you to do it. That is what he meant when he said confess with your mouth and believe in your heart. We must understand that Paul is saying nothing different than Moses when he stated that we may hear it and do it; it should be in your heart that you do it. Through reading the New Testament, it should give you clarity of what the Old Testament meant, and by going back to the source (Old Testament) it should give you clarity of the New Testament writings.

"For the grace of God that bringeth salvation hath appeared to all men, Teaching us that, denying ungodliness and worldly lusts, we should live soberly, righteously, and godly, in this present world (Titus 2:11-12)."

The verse goes on to state in Titus 2:13-14, "Looking for

that blessed hope, and the glorious appearing of the great God and our Saviour Jesus Christ; Who gave himself for us, that he might redeem us from all iniquity, and purify unto himself a peculiar people, zealous of good works." According to this verse, the grace of God should influence a man to the point of him becoming zealous to do good. It is that influence that brings salvation.

Finally, to get the promises of God, you have to repent. If you don't, Jesus said ye shall all likewise perish: Luke 13:4-5, "Or those eighteen, upon whom the tower in Siloam fell, and slew them, think ye that they were sinners above all men that dwelt in Jerusalem? I tell you, Nay: but, except ye repent, ye shall all likewise perish."

This necessity of repenting was made clear to Paul when the Lord appeared to him in Acts 26:16-20.

> "And I said . . . I have appeared unto thee for this purpose, to make thee a minister and a witness both of these things which thou hast seen, and of those things in the which I will appear unto thee; Delivering thee from the people, and from the Gentiles, unto whom now I send thee, To open their eyes, and to turn them from darkness to light, and from the power of Satan unto God, that they may receive forgiveness of sins, and inheritance among them which are sanctified by faith that is in me. Whereupon, O king Agrippa, I was not disobedient unto the heavenly vision: But shewed first unto them of Damascus, and at Jerusalem, and throughout all the coasts of Judaea, and then to the Gentiles, that they should

repent and turn to God, and do works meet for re-pentance."

This is what Paul preached. He told them to turn to God, to repent of their ways, and do works meet for repentance. God is no longer looking for an animal for you to kill for your sins. Jesus said, "I will have mercy and not sacrifice (Matt. 9:13)." Jesus is saying in this passage that he is commanding all sinners to repent, and a slain animal is not acceptable anymore.

But what does he require from each and every one of us? This question is answered in Rom. 12:1, " . . . present your bodies a living sacrifice, holy, acceptable unto God, which is your reasonable service." So, you should start cleaning up your lives. He wants a sacrifice that is living and not a dead animal.

CHAPTER 3

Grace for Grace

When you see how grace is used in the Bible, it is really contrary to how churches use it today. Grace has never been something that lets you by for wrongdoing. There is not one time in the Bible that says, "God lets you by for wrong behavior."

In this chapter, I will show you:

1) How grace has gotten off course

2) The effect of the proper use of grace

3) The intent of God when he gave grace to mankind

4) How grace has been disannulled through the misunderstanding of people

If you look in a modern dictionary, you will see that one of the definitions of grace is the theological definition, which is unmerited favor. This is how churches define grace. In the dictionary you will see a phrase like (*in Christian belief*) in parenthesis in front of the theological meaning. That means that the churches have accepted grace to mean unmerited favor, and so the dictionary has to recognize the churches' definition. Therefore, the definition that the dictionary often uses is really the theological meaning that the churches have given it.

In the world today, grace is defined as charm, attractiveness with excellence; or refinement in movement. For example, when someone is in a competition, whether it is figure skating or dunking a basketball, you would not call that person graceful if they fell down or missed a dunk, neither would the judges score them high, which would reflect a graceful act. It is commonly called "lacking grace" because of the falling down, or the mishap.

Three Scriptures About Grace to Consider

"But grow in grace . . ." (2 Peter 3:18)

". . . continue in the grace of God" (Acts 13:43)

". . . fallen from grace" (Galatians 5:4)

I want to use these three illustrations to give you a clear understanding of grace in its true form. We see that Peter instructed the church in 2 Peter 3:18 which reads, "But grow in grace, and in the knowledge of our Lord and Saviour Jesus Christ. To him be glory both now and for ever. Amen." Peter emphasized the importance of growing in grace, which is not understood today. For example, when growing in grace in the natural world, someone may have a child that socializes with friends that are engaged with drugs, violence, and have dropped out of school. As a result of this lifestyle, the child makes zeroes on his report card. When this child begins to move away from the environment to study his school assignments, the child will gain grace in the sight of his parents for this improvement. The child will continue to grow in the grace of his parents because his grades went from zero to fifty. The child will continue to grow in grace of his parents if his grades continue to increase, even if the increase is minor. In Matthew 13:8, Jesus spoke about the seed that fell on good ground; they all brought forth good fruit. Some not as much as the other, but they all started to do better. Now if the child's grades continue at fifty each semester, or fall back to forty, the child would not find favor in the sight of his parents for this lack of improvement. This is to say doing better is always good or graceful in the sight of God. But if better does not improve then the same performance starts to disintegrate, and that which was good becomes poor and not acceptable.

Paul explains this process very clearly in Romans 12:2 when he said these words, "And be not conformed to this world: but be ye transformed by the renewing of your mind, that ye may prove what is that good, and acceptable, and perfect, will of God." What God sees as good, often is not acceptable and perfect. God sees faith and repentance as good, but if not added to, it becomes poor and eventually failing. Apostle Peter stated,

> "And beside this, giving all diligence, add to
> your faith virtue; and to virtue knowledge; and to
> knowledge temperance, and to temperance patience;
> and to patience godliness; and to godliness brotherly

kindness; and to brotherly kindness charity . . . But
he that lacketh these things is blind, and cannot see
afar off, and hath forgotten that he was purged from
his old sins" (2 Pet. 1:5-7, 9).

We can see clearly that Peter is saying if you do not add to faith, you will forget the new lifestyle and return to the old; in doing so you fall from grace. Paul speaks of falling from grace in many different ways. He corrected the church in Gal. 5:4, "Christ is become of no effect unto you, whosoever of you are justified by the law; ye are fallen from grace." They had FALLEN FROM GRACE by going back to the rituals of the Law to purify themselves and not being mindful of the doctrine of Christ which he taught.

Hebrews 6:1, "Therefore leaving the principles of the doctrine of Christ, let us go on unto perfection; not laying again the foundation of repentance from dead works, and of faith toward God." As the child falls from the grace of his parents by going back to his old friends, to the drugs and not going to class, so does the Christian that has begun in the faith and goes back to his old ways, he has fallen from grace. We see this example also in Peter, where he explains this return back to the old life. 2 Peter 2:22, "But it is happened unto them according to the true proverb, the dog is turned to his own vomit again; and the sow that was washed to her wallowing in the mire."

God is ever merciful and forgiving for those that repent at any time and call upon his name. So, I urge you to repent and find the grace of God if you have gone astray.

There are examples of men in the Bible who found grace in the sight of God. Genesis 6:8-9 states, "but Noah found grace in the eyes of the Lord. These are the generations of Noah: Noah was a just man and perfect in his generations, and Noah walked with God." These verses explain how Noah found grace in the sight of the Lord because he ordered his lifestyle according to God's commandments. Even so, today, if anyone walks with God and does all that he commands them, without contradiction, will find grace with God. For a New Testament example, we find that Jesus was "full of grace and truth" (John 1:14). This term truly means that all aspects of his life were graceful in the sight of God, and all of his teachings and understanding were completely true. If grace means sloppy living or that any lifestyle is acceptable to God, then Jesus would not have needed it. If grace were meant to excuse wrong behavior, Jesus himself would not have been full of it because he did no wrong.

Now we can clearly understand the statement "by grace you are saved" because grace has been explained correctly. However, mankind has found a way to change the meaning of grace to justify ungodly men by saying, "grace is unmerited favor." This erroneous meaning of grace has been commonly used by clergy and theologians to the extent that it has found itself in modern dictionaries to support this incorrect meaning. The word "grace" comes from the Greek word *charis* (khar'-ece) [Also, "charisma" is a derivative of *charis*], which means graciousness, a gratifying manner or act, the divine influence upon the heart of man, and its reflection in the life of man, and also that their life is ACCEPTABLE, FAVORABLE, and BENEFICIAL to God.

Now let me show you how grace affected the greater Apostle Paul. Paul stated prior to Christ that he was the chief of sinners. In 1 Tim. 1:12-15, Paul said,

> *"And I thank Christ Jesus our Lord, who hath enabled me, for that he counted me faithful, putting me into the ministry; Who was before a blasphemer, and a persecutor, and injurious: but I obtained mercy, because I did it ignorantly in unbelief. And the grace of our Lord was exceeding abundant with faith and love which is in Christ Jesus. This is a faithful saying, and worthy of all acceptation, that Christ Jesus came into the world to save sinners; of whom I am chief."*

This passage is loaded with understanding of grace and mercy. Never make grace and mercy the same; they are different. Misunderstanding grace and mercy has been extremely harmful to the church. Paul mentions mercy and he mentions grace in this Scripture, talking about two different things. He explains mercy when he talked about his sinful lifestyle prior to Christ, being a chief sinner who was completely forgiven, and he explains grace as being empowered by God to become favorable.

Let's go back to chapter one of John's Gospel so you can see what I'm saying.

> *"And the Word was made flesh, and dwelt among us, (and we beheld his glory, the glory as of the only begotten of the Father) full of grace and truth. John bare witness of him, and cried, saying, This was he of whom I spake, He that cometh after me is preferred before me: for he was before me. And of his fullness have all we received, and grace for grace" (John 1:14-16).*

Here he uses the phrase that we receive grace for grace, meaning you receive grace for being graceful. That's just like saying you receive an "A" for doing excellent work.

"For the law was given by Moses, but grace and truth came by Jesus Christ" (John 1:17). We who claim to have grace must acknowledge that we have to walk in truth to receive grace. The truth of God's Word is precisely what Jesus instructs. It's not what any man thinks, or religion says, but rather what God's Word says to all of us.

Now I want to show you the following Scripture, which clearly explains the biblical meaning of grace. "For the grace of God that bringeth salvation hath appeared to all men" (Titus 2:11). Here it is telling you that it comes to every man that exists, but why does not every man have grace? Because when grace comes, this is what it does: "Teaching us that, denying ungodliness and worldly lusts, we should live soberly, righteously, and godly, in this present world" (Titus 2:12). So, grace comes to all men, and it tells you to straighten your life up by denying ungodliness (deny and refuse anything that is not like God). Anything that has something to do with worldly lust, you need to also deny that. And you need to live godly in the world we live in now. Titus 2:13-14 goes on to say, "Looking for that blessed hope, and the glorious appearing of the great God and our Saviour Jesus Christ; Who gave himself for us, that he might redeem us from all iniquity, and purify unto himself a peculiar people, zealous of good works."

He said in verse 14 to "purify a people," meaning grace came to teach people how to live a purified life after being cleansed by Jesus's blood. Not to let a people by with wrongdoing, but grace came to clean your mind and your ways, and also your actions. That verse also said, "zealous of good works." See, grace makes you excited about doing what is good. Grace comes to all, it is available for all, and God will not refuse giving it to any who desire it. But everyone who desires it must have the mindset to be zealous of doing what is good.

For a man that has been accustomed to doing wrong, he needs to receive the Holy Spirit to continue this new life. *"And, being assembled together with them, commanded them that they should not depart from Jerusalem, but wait for the promise of the Father, which, saith he, ye have heard of me" (Acts 1:4).* I want you to look at this very clearly. Notice that Jesus had come to the disciples after his death and the promise still had not yet come. Churches believe that all you have to do is believe that Jesus died and rose again. No! These men knew he rose again, and they had not received the promise at this point!

"For John truly baptized with water; but ye shall be baptized with the Holy Ghost not many days hence" (Acts 1:5). Now he is telling them that the Holy Ghost is going to come upon them. I'm going to explain how you should know you have it—don't deceive yourself. I was determined I was not going to get off of my knees until God made a change in my life. Through continual study of the Bible, <u>I realized the reason it took me so long to receive the Holy Ghost was that I wasn't ready to give up everything that was not like God.</u> *Acts 5:32, states, ". . . also the Holy Ghost, whom God hath given to them that obey him."* From this verse, I learned every man must be willing to completely obey God to receive the Holy Ghost. Now if you are not obeying God, do not claim the Holy Ghost.

Jesus said, "But ye shall receive power, after that the Holy Ghost is come upon you: and ye shall be witnesses unto me both in Jerusalem, and in all Judaea, and in Samaria, and unto the uttermost part of the earth" (Acts 1:8). Here, all one hundred twenty people were waiting on something after Jesus's death and resurrection. They still knew they needed something else. And if you are honest with yourself, and you know that you haven't done more than believe, you need something else too!

Don't let any preacher tell you that you have it all right when you know your own mind, and you know what is working on the inside of you when you're by yourself. You need power from on high! So, I tarried and prayed for the Holy Ghost, and it did not come into me until I made a commitment to God to obey him. The moment I gave up everything, my faith increased to believe God, being that I was no longer holding anything back from him. By faith he came inside of me, and he delivered me from my old lifestyle. The nightclub didn't see me anymore; the old girlfriends I used to call, I didn't call them anymore. Instead, I began to be a witness and preach to others about this change of lifestyle as Peter did upon receiving the Holy Ghost in Acts 2:37, "Now when they heard this, they were pricked in their heart, and said unto Peter and to the rest of the apostles, Men and brethren, what shall we do?"

Your question should be, "What shall I do?" He said, ". . . they were pricked in their hearts." So, if you really want to be saved, you have to get serious in your heart and say, "I want a changed life."

Let's see what Peter instructed them to do. *"Then Peter said unto them, Repent, and be baptized every one of you in the name of Jesus Christ for the remission of sins, and ye shall receive the gift of the Holy Ghost" (Acts 2:38).* He is telling them to change their lives. <u>He did not tell them, "repeat this prayer after me, and you're saved," and he didn't tell them, "say these words, and we believe you got born again."</u> Since Peter did not say that why do we accept such statements that are not written in the Bible to be correct? Ask your preacher, "Where is it written in the Bible if I say these words then I'm saved?" It's not there! However, the following quotation is in the Scripture. Romans 10:9 states, "That if thou shalt confess with thy mouth the Lord Jesus, and shalt believe in thine heart that God hath raised him from the dead, thou shalt be saved." But this is speaking in terms of you making Jesus your Lord from your heart, which will result in you repenting to follow his lifestyle, not with just words spoken.

Paul also talked about this spirit of grace. Paul reflected on when he was weak and struggling; he said that he sought God three times about it, and God said in 2 Corinthians 12:9, "My grace is sufficient for thee: for my strength is made perfect in weakness." Paul said, ". . . for when I am weak, then am I strong." What he is saying is when I got down on my knees, and I felt that I needed God, and I relied upon God. The grace of God was stronger in me, not weaker in me. He said that I became stronger. Paul never stated that he continued to fall down to get up, but he spoke how grace made him stronger. Paul also said these words, "Finally, my brethren, be strong in the Lord, and in the power of his might" (Eph. 6:10). *We can be strong in God*!

Peter also said these words in Acts 2:40, *"And with many other words did he testify and exhort, saying, Save yourselves from this untoward generation."* Here is Peter saying, save yourselves, but you are often told (incorrectly)that you don't have to do anything.

"Then they that gladly received his word were baptized: and the same day there were added unto them about three thousand souls. And they continued steadfastly in the apostles' doctrine and fellowship, and in breaking of bread, and in prayers" (Acts 2:41-42). Notice it says in verse 42, ". . . and they continued steadfastly in the apostles' doctrine." You have to get in the doctrine of what the apostles taught you and not what your religion says, because religion changes all the time. But God said, "I am the LORD and I change not" (Malachi 3:6).

CHAPTER 4

God's Grace Changes and Saves

In the beginning, it was grace that saved Noah.

> *"And GOD saw that the wickedness of man was great in the earth, and that every imagination of the thoughts of his heart was only evil continually. And it repented the LORD that he had made man on the earth, and it grieved him at his heart. And the LORD said, I will destroy man whom I have created from the face of the earth; both man, and beast, and the creeping thing, and the fowls of the air; for it repenteth me that I have made them. But Noah found grace in the eyes of the LORD" (Gen. 6:5-8).*

This scripture clearly states that Noah was viewed favorably by God! Now, why did Noah find grace but the rest of the world did not? Churches today teach that the wicked and ungodly are rewarded with grace, and the worse you are, the more grace you get. Let's see how Noah gets grace . . .

"These are the generations of Noah: Noah was a just man and perfect in his generations, and Noah walked with God" (Gen. 6:9). Here is an individual who has made up his mind to do what God said, and this is why Noah found grace in the eyes of the Lord. Noah did not find grace by being unfavorable with God, but rather by being obedient to God. Most people understand that grace means favor, but today's theology has varied from the etymology (the origin) of grace. The sad thing about it is, the only people who have changed the meaning of this word to suit their doctrine is the church. Today's Bible scholars teach that grace is unmerited favor. But from the beginning, it was not so. There is no such thing as unmerited favor in the Bible.

Look in your dictionary, and you will see that synonyms of grace are excellence, polished, sanctified, and holy. Make sure you look under the original meaning of grace, not under the theological meaning. Grace is favor, but it's a deserved favor, by being submissive and committing yourself to God. This was the meaning of it every time it was used in the Bible.

The Bible says Lot found grace when he left Sodom. The Bible also says that Lot was a righteous man dwelling among those wicked homosexuals. "For that righteous man dwelling among them, in seeing and hearing, vexed his righteous soul from day to day with their unlawful deeds" (2 Pet. 2:8). Once Lot got ready to leave, he asked the angel, "If I found grace in your sight, can you let me go to Zoar, as it is a closer city." And the angel told him, "You have found grace, so I will prepare that city for you." (Gen. 19:19-21). Lot found grace because he was one committed to God. If grace were like it is believed to be nowadays, all the wicked people of

Sodom would have lived, and the righteous man would have been lost for attempting to follow God's commandments. Rather we see Lots wife fell from grace by refusing the commandment of God not to look back. Lot and his two daughters continued in the grace of God by not looking back. The Bible says in 2 Peter 2:9, "The Lord knoweth how to deliver the godly out of temptations, and to reserve the unjust unto the day of judgment to be punished." This is a prime example of God delivering the godly out of temptation and brining the ungodly into judgement.

God said, "In the latter days, I will pour out my Spirit upon all flesh" (Joel 2:28). Before the latter days, God only poured his Spirit out on a few people; the prophets had it, i.e., David and Samuel. God had grace upon these men, and they had the Spirit of God. Samson had it to do great exploits until he started to sin by being with Delilah and being rebellious to God. The Bible says the spirit of the Lord departed from Saul, so he fell from grace and became like a normal man.

Notice when David had sinned. The thing he was concerned about was not falling from God's grace. David said, "Cast me not away from thy presence; and take not thy holy spirit from me" (Ps. 51:11).

Now, this is when Samuel was about to anoint King Saul as king: "Then Samuel took a vial of oil, and poured it upon his head, and kissed him, and said, Is it not because the LORD hath anointed thee to be captain over his inheritance?" (1 Sam. 10:1).

> *"After that thou shalt come to the hill of God, where is the garrison of the Philistines: and it shall come to pass, when thou art come thither to the city, that thou shalt meet a company of prophets coming down from the high place with a psaltery, and a tabret, and a pipe, and a harp, before them; and they shall prophesy: And the Spirit of the LORD* [or you can use the spirit of grace] *will come upon thee, and thou shalt prophesy with them, and shalt be turned into another man" (1 Sam. 10:5-6).*

He's saying that the Spirit of God will turn you into another man; it will change you from hatred to love.

"And it was so, that when he had turned his back to go from Samuel, God gave him another heart: and all those signs came to pass that day" (1 Sam. 10:9). Notice he said God gave him another heart. This is why David prayed, "Create in me a clean heart." David knew what the Spirit of God would do; it changes the mind and the heart of the man. He didn't say, God, just let me go back to church and dance! He said, God I want my heart changed. I want to be new on the inside. David said create in me a clean heart and renew a right spirit in me. He can renew it in you even if you lost it. David knew he had done wrong, so he asked God for a new spirit.

So, Saul became a new man. He also started to prophesy and to live a new life. At first, he was just a normal person but then began to become compassionate, loving, and meek just like God, and it was because the Spirit of God came upon him—that power that Jesus said that God had promised to all of us in this time.

You would find in the Bible where Saul became envious of David, and the Spirit of God will not abide in an unclean temple. The early church understood that the Spirit of God will not abide in an unclean temple. Do you know why this is so?

"And every spirit that confesseth not that Jesus Christ is come in the flesh is not of God: and this is that spirit of antichrist" (1 John 4:3). This means that you are claiming the Holy Spirit, but your life doesn't bear witness that Christ is in you. You speak in tongues, but you can't stop fighting, and you can't get cussing out of your mouth. You don't have a lick of the Holy Ghost! When Christ comes in you, the Bible says the body is dead because of sin, but the spirit is life because of righteousness!

"But if the Spirit of him that raised up Jesus from the dead dwell in you, he that raised up Christ from the dead shall also quicken your mortal bodies by his Spirit that dwelleth in you!" (Rom. 8:11). It also says in Romans 8:9, "Now if any man have not the Spirit of Christ, he is none of his." This is all Paul's teaching in the book of Romans.

So, Saul began to walk in a godly manner, but you see later the Bible says the Spirit of God departed from Saul, and an evil spirit began to trouble him. When the Spirit of God departed from this kind and humble man, he became so vicious he started trying to kill David. We clearly see that King Saul was not strong or good (neither are we) without God's grace upon him. Here's another example of God's willingness to help and change a struggling people, giving them power to live a pleasing life to him.

> "Moreover the word of the LORD came unto me, saying, Son of man, when the house of Israel dwelt in their own land, they defiled it by their own way and by their doings: their way was before me as the uncleanness of a removed woman. Wherefore I poured my fury upon them for the blood that they had shed upon the land, and for their idols wherewith they had polluted it: And I scattered them among the heathen, and they were dispersed through the countries: according to their way and according to their doings I judged them. And when they entered unto the heathen, whither they went, they profaned my holy name, when they said to them, These are the people of the LORD, and are gone forth out of his land" (Ezek. 36:16-20).

Here's an example of people mocking falling Christians, publicizing their wrong by putting it all over the news. God saw all the shame his people suffered. For there are many people that really have a desire to serve God, but not always make the mark. Wherever they went, the people would just disannul every good thing they would do, the testimonies they would have, and the songs they sang. The heathens took what they were doing and just made mockery out of them.

> "But I had pity for mine holy name, which the house of Israel had profaned among the heathen, whither they went. Therefore say unto the house of Israel, Thus saith the Lord GOD; I do not this for your sakes, O house of Israel, but for mine holy name's sake, which ye have profaned among the heathen, whither ye went. And I will sanctify my great name, which was profaned among the heathen, which ye have profaned in the midst of them; and the heathen shall know that I am the LORD, saith the Lord GOD, when I shall be sanctified in you before their eyes" (Ezek. 36:21-23).

God is saying I'm going to come inside of you and be sanctified inside of you, and they will witness this changed life I am about to bring into the house of Israel. It will not be your doing, because you can't do it by yourself. You can stop killing, but you can't get hatred out of your heart; God has to get it out of your heart. You can stop fornicating, but you can't get a lustful desire out of your heart; God has to get it out of your heart.

"For I will take you from among the heathen, and gather you out of all countries, and will bring you into your own land" (Ezek. 36:24). First, you have to come out from among the world. You can't stay among that wicked lifestyle and think God is going to change you in the midst of it.

"Then will I sprinkle clean water upon you, and ye shall be

clean: from all your filthiness, and from all your idols, will I cleanse you" (Ezek. 36:25). This is what baptism is all about. You are baptized for the remission of sin. When you are baptized in the name of Jesus, he sees you as being put to death. The old man is dead now—the old man that used to steal, rob, commit adultery, and curse has been put away and buried. When you come out of that water, you are supposed to come up with a new faith and a new life.

"A new heart also will I give you, and a new spirit (this is the spirit of grace) will I put within you: and I will take away the stony heart out of your flesh, and I will give you an heart of flesh" (Ezek. 36:26). What does God mean he is going to give you a new heart? He's not going to give you a new heart as in the muscle, but he is going to give you a new, clean mind. So, you're not going to remember and have a pressing issue to go back to the things you're trying to leave because your mind is going to be changed.

"And I will put my spirit within you, and cause you to walk in my statutes, and ye shall keep my judgments, and do them" (Ezek. 36:27). You need to have this experience. If not, you will keep on falling and blundering over the same thing. You have to get this new spirit in you. This new Spirit made Saul turn into a new man and to prophesy. It made David strong enough to kill a lion with his hands. That same Spirit made Samson so strong he took a donkey's jawbone and killed a thousand Philistines, and they had swords and shields. Paul said this same Spirit raised Jesus Christ from the dead. This Spirit has the power to take a man who was dead and make him alive again. So why do you believe it can't take lust out of your heart?

Notice the Scripture says it will "cause you to walk in my statutes, and ye shall keep my judgments and do them." So here is God saying when this Spirit gets in you, it will cause you to walk in his statutes, which means to walk in a manner that is in representation of God's personality, ways, judgement and his conduct. This Spirit is going to cause you to act like God. I'm talking about you being free from sin, free from drugs, free from adultery, free from sodomy. I'm talking about you being a new creature!

God said it like this in Ezekiel 36:31, "Then shall ye remember your own evil ways, and your doings that were not good, and shall lothe yourselves in your own sight for your iniquities and for your abominations." You would now be ashamed of the bad things you used to brag about. That is the grace of God that will come on the inside of you.

This is the transition from the old covenant to the new and why God changed it: "For the law having a shadow of good things to come, and not the very image of the things, can never with those sacrifices which they offered year by year continually make the comers thereunto perfect" (Heb. 10:1). The Law could never make the people coming into that covenant perfect by killing bulls and goats.

"For then would they not have ceased to be offered? Because that the worshippers once purged should have had no more conscience of sins" (Heb. 10:2). Notice he said, "For then would they not have ceased to be offered?" This means if the sacrifices could have made the people perfect, God would not have stopped the offering of the bulls and goats once the worshipper was purged.

"But in those sacrifices there is a remembrance again made of sins every year. For it is not possible that the blood of bulls and of goats should take away sins. Wherefore when he cometh into the world (he is talking about the new covenant), he saith, Sacrifice and offering thou wouldest not, but a body hast thou prepared me" (Heb. 10:3-5). When you see the words "he saith," you can always find it back in the Old Testament.

"Then said I, Lo, I come (in the volume of the book it is written of me) to do thy will, O God" (Heb. 10:7). This was taken from Psalm 40, so let's go back and see where he got this from: "Sacrifice and offering thou didst not desire; mine ears hast thou opened: burnt offering and sin offering hast thou not required. Then said I, Lo, I come: in the volume of the book it is written of me, I delight to do thy will, O my God: yea, thy law is within my heart" (Psalm 40:6-8). In verse 6, the psalmist is saying God has never liked sacrifices for your sins.

So, we understand that God has never wanted the burnt offerings and sacrifices for your wrongdoing, but he wanted you to have in your heart to do his will and not have to kill something for you! See, the churches are teaching law and preach against law all the time, because they constantly talk about how Jesus died for you (speaking of all of your sins that you have committed and will commit). That's what it was under the Law. But under grace, the Law is planted in the heart to do God's will.

"Then said I, Lo, I come: in the volume of the book it is written of me, I delight to do thy will, O my God: yea, thy law is within my heart. I have preached righteousness in the great congregation: lo, I have not refrained my lips, O LORD, thou knowest" (Ps. 40:7-9). What he is saying is I come now in this new covenant, not to keep killing bulls and goats, and Christ keep dying. But I came to die once for their sin! And I'm going to put the whole book in their hearts, and they are going to do God's will!

"For if we sin willfully after that we have received the knowledge of the truth, there remaineth no more sacrifice for sins" (Heb. 10:26). Now he is telling you that God has given you the truth, and God doesn't want you to sin willfully. God wants you to act right because Christ is not getting back on the cross for you.

So, let's go back to Hebrews 10:5-6, "Wherefore when he cometh into the world, he saith, Sacrifice and offering thou wouldest not, but a body hast thou prepared me: In burnt offerings and sacrifices for sin thou hast had no pleasure." We understand God was tired of them killing the bulls and the goats for their sins. Now God wants to prepare your body to serve him. He wants to prepare your heart to be right, and he wants to clean your mind to love your neighbor.

"Then said he, Lo, I come to do thy will, O God. He taketh away the first that he may establish the second" (Heb. 10:9). Now above in verses 5-6, he said, " . . . in burnt offerings and sacrifices for sin thou hast had no pleasure" which was offered by the law (offerings, sacrifices, killing the bulls and goats). He says in verse 9, "Lo, I come to do thy will, O God. He taketh away the first, (the first was offering the burnt offerings and sacrifices) that he may establish the second." The killing of bulls, goats, and sheep continued, but nobody stopped sinning, so he took away the sacrifices and established a man's heart to do what is right. Let him clean your heart and establish your mind!

He took away the first that he may establish the second. What he is really saying is, if I keep letting you kill bulls and goats for your wrong, if I keep letting you rely upon a sacrifice or anything to get you free, you will never get it right.

"By the which will we are sanctified through the offering of the body of Jesus Christ once for all" (Heb. 10:10).

"Having therefore, brethren, boldness to enter into the holiest by the blood of Jesus, By a new and living way, which he hath consecrated for us, through the veil, that is to say, his flesh" (Heb. 10:19-20). Now notice what he said in verse 20—"By a new and living way." You have to live this. It is not supposed to be the "Jesus-did-it-all way". No, you are entering into a new way where you have to live it now. If I can live it, you can too. Tell me. <u>What sin do you have to commit to live?</u> NONE. Every sin you do is because you desire to do it. Whether it be desires related to adultery, homosexuality, lesbianism, thievery, lying, drunkenness, etc. they will all put you on a pathway to hell. (1 Cor 6:9-10)

However it states in Hebrews 10:21-22, *"And having an high priest over the house of God; Let us draw near with a true heart in full assurance of faith, having our hearts sprinkled from an evil conscience, and our bodies washed with pure water"* . When he says having our hearts sprinkled from an evil conscience, God is telling us, that he will remove the memory with the urge to sin from our minds. He went on to say, "and our bodies washed with pure water;" meaning through baptism your body is cleansed from all previous sins. This is likened unto dirty clothes after being washed in cleaning detergent should be free from stain.

"Let us hold fast the profession of our faith without wavering (for he is faithful that promised)" (Heb. 10:23). He is saying, let us not keep stumbling and falling.

"And let us consider one another to provoke unto love and to good works: Not forsaking the assembling of ourselves together, as the manner of some is; but exhorting one another: and so much the more, as ye see the day approaching. For if we sin willfully after that we have received the knowledge of the truth, there remaineth no more sacrifice for sins" (Heb. 10:24-26). In verse 26, what he is saying is if you continue to sin like you did before, God is not accepting bulls and goats and calves or any more sacrifices for sin.

What happens when you continue to live a life of sin after baptism? Hebrews 10:27 tells us what to look for: "But a certain fearful looking for of judgment and fiery indignation, which shall devour the adversaries." Indignation means that God is upset with you.

"He that despised Moses' law died without mercy under two or three witnesses: Of how much sorer punishment, suppose ye, shall he be thought worthy, who hath trodden under foot the Son of God, and hath counted the blood of the covenant, wherewith he was sanctified, an unholy thing, and hath done despite unto the Spirit of grace?" (Heb. 10:28-29). Here the writer is saying when you do despite unto the spirit of grace, you are supposed to be looking for a worse punishment than under the Law of Moses. "For we know him that hath said, Vengeance belongeth unto me, I will recompense, saith the Lord. And again, The Lord shall judge his people" (Heb.

10:30).

What happens when a righteous man has given his life to God, and he ends up committing a sin? I have committed some sin since I got saved. But when that happened to me the brokenness of my heart led me on my face to weep. I did not have to go and offer up a sacrifice. The acknowledgment of my error, the conviction of my heart led me to be sorrowful to repentance for what happened, and that drew me nearer to God. And God washed my mind, cleaned me up, and started me right off again in a new way. So, he is still merciful, and he is still compassionate.

CHAPTER 5

How God Defines Unbelief

The Bible says in Revelation 22:12, "And, behold, I come quickly; and my reward is with me, to give every man according as his work shall be." Many people are saying today that you do not do works to be saved, but Jesus said my reward is with me, and I will reward every one of you according to what your work shall be. Now, he's not saying you can work yourself into heaven. You have to be working according to his plan in your life and committed to the purpose that God has for you in life. Apart from doing what God says, and apart from carrying out God's order, all of the things that you claim as faith in the sight of God are classified as unbelief.

I want to say this again. All of the things you failed to do, that you know God has said and commanded you to do, in the sight of God, he classifies them as unbelief. In this chapter, I will answer the following:

1) What is true faith in God?

2) Why are we saved by faith?

3) What makes faith save us?

Many times, we are told that faith is something you believe

in your head, that there is a living and existing God, and that's sufficient enough. That is error. This is what the Bible says: James 2:19, "Thou believest that there is one God; thou doest well: the devils also believe, and tremble." So, if believing in God apart from commitment to God were satisfactory then the devils would be saved.

This is where Jesus began to upbraid many of the cities wherein most of his mighty works were done. You hear so many people talk about Jesus going around the sinners, which he did. If you read Matthew 11, it really gives you clarity on how Jesus went to sinners. They believed him enough to get a miracle but didn't believe him enough to repent.

Matthew 11:20, "Then began he to upbraid the cities wherein most of his mighty works were done, because they repented not." In the cities that he was about to upbraid, you find that there were people who had faith.

Matthew 11:21, "Woe unto thee, Chorazin! woe unto thee, Bethsaida! for if the mighty works, which were done in you, had been done in Tyre and Sidon, they would have repented long ago in sackcloth and ashes." Chorazin was a place where Jesus did many mighty works; this is where the centurion came and asked Jesus just to send the word, and his servant would be healed. They believed to receive all types of miracles, and he even fed the five thousand, and they sat down to eat. But the Bible says he began to upbraid these cities because their faith didn't cause them to repent.

Sometimes there would be so many sinners come to meet him that they couldn't get in through the door; the door would be jammed when they heard Jesus would be in town, but they were there for the fish and the loaves. They were there for a miracle, but they were not there to follow this new lifestyle that Jesus was bringing and presenting to them. But they would gather around him, and in one instance, when they couldn't get in, they went on top of the roof and broke the roof up to let a man down who had been sick with palsy. Matthew 9:2, "Jesus seeing their faith said unto the sick of the palsy; Son, be of good cheer; thy sins be forgiven thee." But Jesus never saw these people change their lives. They only got miracles; they only got healings and got bread to feed themselves. But they did not change their lifestyle. So now he is letting them know that he has performed miracles for them, but it's woe unto them now because they are not repenting.

Matthew 11:23, "And thou, Capernaum, which art exalted unto heaven, shalt be brought down to hell: for if the mighty works, which have been done in thee, had been done in Sodom, it would have remained until this day." Capernaum was a very prosperous city. They had many wheat fields, and it was centrally located in a strategic place such that most of the travel by water to the western and eastern side of Israel was done through Capernaum.

Matthew 11:24, "But I say unto you, That it shall be more tolerable for the land of Sodom in the day of judgment, than for thee." Here Jesus is saying you have seen the miracles, and you have seen the healings, but all you have done is treasure up wrath for yourself because you have not turned to me and have not repented of your sins. I want to share with you what God really classifies as unbelief.

How many of you know that Moses believed and trusted in God? Moses saw him face to face, and he gave Moses the commandments. But I can show you where God told Moses that he was not going to enter into the promised land because of unbelief. See, we have to understand what God classifies as unbelief. The fact that you believe in an existing God does not make you a believer, but how you respond to the existing God.

The Bible said this about Abraham in James 2:21, "Was not Abraham our father justified by works, when he had offered Isaac his son upon the altar?" He was not justified by faith until he responded to what God said. What God commanded him to do was very difficult, and by faith he went to offer up his son to God. The Bible said that's when he was justified by works. We are those who are justified by faith, but how many of you are responding to what God told you to do?

We are dealing with what is classified as unbelief in God's

eyesight, so I'm going to show you an example of how God classified Moses as an unbeliever, and what effect it had on Moses. The following passage is when the children of Israel didn't have any water, and they wanted water:

Numbers 20:7-12:

> *"And the Lord spake unto Moses, saying, Take the rod, and gather thou the assembly together, thou, and Aaron thy brother, and speak ye unto the rock before their eyes; and it shall give forth his water, and thou shalt bring forth to them water out of the rock: so thou shalt give the congregation and their beasts drink. And Moses took the rod from before the Lord, as he commanded him. And Moses and Aaron gathered the congregation together before the rock, and he said unto them, Hear now, ye rebels; must we fetch you water out of this rock? And Moses lifted up his hand, and with his rod he smote the rock twice: and the water came out abundantly, and the congregation drank, and their beasts also. And the Lord spake unto Moses and Aaron, Because ye believed me not, to sanctify me in the eyes of the children of Israel, therefore ye shall not bring this congregation into the land which I have given them."*

God was saying to Moses, You believed me not that I required sanctification, and I required holiness. Hebrews 12:14, "Follow peace with all men, and holiness, without which no man shall see the Lord:" Here was Moses knowing how great God was, who had talked with God, had received the commandments from God, yet allowed his temper to get in the way and God said, You didn't believe me in this category.

Are there categories of life that you omit in your faith? Do you omit paying your tithes? Do you omit loving your neighbor as yourself? Do you believe that you only have to believe in an existing God, and that's all that matters? Do you believe as the Lord has commanded us to do in Ephesians? Ephesians 6:11, "Put on the whole armor of God, that ye may be able to stand against the wiles of the devil."

You must believe every word that comes out of the mouth of God and not just portions of the Word. For example, Matthew 21:42, "The stone which the builders rejected, the same is become the head of the corner: this is the Lord's doing, and it is marvelous in our eyes?" To get more understanding of that passage, go with me to 1 Peter 2:5, "Ye also, as lively stones, are built up a spiritual house, an holy priesthood, to offer up spiritual sacrifices, acceptable to God by Jesus Christ." When I'm preaching to you the Word, I'm throwing at you lively stones to build up a spiritual house.

It went on to say, in 1 Peter 2:7-8, "But unto them which be disobedient, the stone which the builders disallowed, the same is made the head of the corner, And a stone of stumbling, and a rock of offence, even to them which stumble at the word, being disobedient: whereunto also they were appointed."

Again, when I'm throwing you out God's Word, I'm throwing you out stones to build a spiritual house. But when you get to the point where you reject any parts of this Word, you are rejecting a stone that should be included in your building. And when you reject that stone, it becomes the chief and most important stone that you need to cause your building to continue to be erected. If you reject that stone, then it causes you to fall, and it becomes a weakness in your life. That stone can be something simple like not apologizing for wrong or not forgiving your brother of their trespass. We think if we're saved, we can avoid the brother in church and don't talk with the brother at church! But the Bible says in Matthew 6:15, "But if ye forgive not men their trespasses, neither will your Father forgive your trespasses." The devil wants you to believe that doesn't really matter. Yes, it does! When you reject that stone, it becomes the chief cornerstone in your building.

Numbers 20:12, "And the Lord spake unto Moses and Aaron, Because ye believed me not, to sanctify me in the eyes of the children of Israel, therefore ye shall not bring this congregation into the land which I have given them." Did Moses have grace? Yes, he did. Did Moses have favor with God? Yes, he did. But God did not allow Moses to escape when he commanded him to walk in a certain capacity or a certain way. This hurt Moses very much. He was crying and asking God to let him in to the point God said, "I'm not going to let you in. Joshua, your servant, is going to bring them in. I want you to encourage him."

I wouldn't want God to rip something from me because of a part of my personality that I'm determined to hold on to, when I know he is determined, and he requires me to walk in a certain way.

Now we can clearly see that although Moses was a man whom God had put in charge, he still did not let him get by because of favor or because he believed in the existing God.

Hebrews 4:7, ". . . To day, after so long a time; as it is said, To day if ye will hear his voice, harden not your hearts." What he is saying here is when you hear the message of God, whether it's coming from a minister, your mother, or a saint in the church, harden not your heart.

Hebrews 3:12, "Take heed, brethren, lest there be in any of you an evil heart of unbelief, in departing from the living God." He is saying, when you depart from serving God or doing God's will, God calls that heart you have a heart of unbelief. Now it doesn't matter what your preacher has said or what's going on in your mind, it's how God judges your heart. When you walk away from him, that's an evil heart of unbelief. You believe that God exists, you believe that God will come back, and even while you're thinking that Jesus came to die for your sins, you back up from obeying him. God said that's an evil heart of unbelief.

Hebrews 3:13, "But exhort one another daily, while it is

called To day; lest any of you be hardened through the deceitfulness of sin." Our hearts become hardened when there are sins in our lives that we don't want to cast away. We want to hold on to God, but we want to hold on to some sins that we know are forbidden by God.

Why does God call it a heart of unbelief? The Bible said it like this in 1 Corinthians 6:9a, "Know ye not that the unrighteous shall not inherit the kingdom of God?" Now God will tell you that the unrighteous will not inherit the kingdom of God, but you will have that unrighteous life and somehow believe you're going to slide in anyhow. So, you really don't believe what he is saying.

In 1 Corinthians 6:9b-10 it continues, "Be not deceived: neither fornicators, nor idolaters, nor adulterers, nor effeminate, nor abusers of themselves with mankind, Nor thieves, nor covetous, nor drunkards, nor revilers, nor extortioners, shall inherit the kingdom of God." But a heart of unbelief says, "I can do those things, and God still loves me and will allow me to escape," even though he has never said he will allow his love to excuse you. But your unbelieving heart will make you hold on to wrong, still believing God will excuse you. You believe you can be unrighteous and still make it in. That is called unbelief.

Believing in God does not mean believing beyond what God says or fabricating your own thoughts or methods of salvation. I don't care how mighty you make God or make Jesus. Believing in

God is when you take the words of Jesus or the Word of God and trust in what he said as what he said. That's when you are believing in him.

Hebrews 3:15 says:

> *"While it is said, To day if ye will hear his voice, harden not your hearts, as in the provocation. For some, when they had heard, did provoke: howbeit not all that came out of Egypt by Moses. But with whom was he grieved forty years? was it not with them that had sinned, whose carcases fell in the wilderness? And to whom swore he that they should not enter into his rest, but to them that believed not?"*

What he first said was to them who had sinned, then he went on and said to them who believed not. So, what he is really trying to tell you is that people who don't believe in God the way that he tells us to believe will continue to sin and believe that God is going to let them by. But he says the day you hear his voice, harden not your heart.

So, we see that they could not enter in because of unbelief, and we understand that the Bible correlates sin with unbelief. We have to understand that there will be a judgment when we leave this earth.

The Gospel of Luke,16:22-24, talks about a rich man dying and a poor man dying.

> *"And it came to pass, that the beggar died,*

and was carried by the angels into Abraham's bo-
som: the rich man also died, and was buried; And in
hell he lift up his eyes, being in torments, and seethe
Abraham afar off, and Lazarus in his bosom. And he
cried and said, Father Abraham, have mercy on me,
and send Lazarus, that he may dip the tip of his fin-
ger in water, and cool my tongue; for I am tormented
in this flame."

Luke 16:27-28, "Then he said, I pray thee therefore, father, that thou wouldest send him to my father's house: For I have five brethren; that he may testify unto them, lest they also come into this place of torment."

The thing that was so amazing to me and so telling is that this man was dead, and his body left on the earth to be buried, and the man himself had not changed. Now Lazarus was one who desired crumbs off the rich man's table. When the rich man died and saw Lazarus in heaven while he was in hell, he still felt that he should have dominion over Lazarus. When he recognized Lazarus, he felt he ought to tell him what to do and that Lazarus should go do it. How could he have the audacity to send this man back to slave for him like he used to in the earth? One thing it shows us clearly is that your mindset and your attitude and personality will not change. Death doesn't change the personality that you have. If you are vicious and mean-spirited, you will be the same out of this body. That's why you have to clean your life up while you're alive, through obedience to the Word of God, as Jesus said in John 15:3, "**Now** ye are clean through the word which I have spoken unto you."

Also, Peter said in 1 Peter 1:22, "Seeing ye have purified your souls in obeying the truth through the Spirit unto unfeigned love of the brethren, see that ye love one another with a pure heart fervently." Now we must remember all of these Scriptures are written to believers—unto people who have confessed the Lord. He is talking to people who are claiming the Lord Jesus as their Savior.

Hebrews 4:1, "Let us therefore fear, lest, a promise being left us of entering into his rest, any of you should seem to come short of it." Notice he said some of you seem to come short of it. So yes, Christian people can come short of entering into the rest of God. Christian people can be lost; people who have been in church all their lives. This is why he says in Hebrews 4:2, "For unto us was the gospel preached, as well as unto them: but the word preached did not profit them, not being mixed with faith in them that heard it."

When I preach the word to you, it is important for you to grab what the Word of God says, and you ought to state within yourself that you believe that. For example, in Hebrews 12:12-14, "Wherefore lift up the hands which hang down, and the feeble knees; And make straight paths for your feet, lest that which is lame be turned out of the way; but let it rather be healed. Follow peace with all men, and holiness, without which no man shall see the Lord."

So, what he is saying is you have to get your feet going in straight paths and walk in the right way; lift up your hands that hang down and stop feeling sorry for yourself. Get yourself on the right path. He is talking about a church, people who are going through, and have been hurt and seem to be chastised by the Lord. He is telling them to get themselves together and continue to trust God and continue to move forward. Stop moping and groping in your sorrows, but get yourselves together, and make straight paths and continue to trust in Jesus Christ.

Hebrews 12:15, "Looking diligently lest any man fail of the grace of God; lest any root of bitterness springing up trouble you, and thereby many be defiled."

Hebrews 12:1, "Wherefore seeing we also are compassed about with so great a cloud of witnesses, let us lay aside every weight, and the sin which doth so easily beset us, and let us run with patience the race that is set before us." Here he is referring to Hebrews 11 and the hardships that the godly people went through and how they were tempted. And he was talking about how they were sawn asunder and slain with the edge of the sword to serve God. Many of them went through hardship, but they never gave up.

Now he says we have all of these witnesses before us. Look at Samson and how he got strong after he came back from what he did. In chapter 11, he talked about how Moses chose to suffer affliction with the people of God. He showed examples of how men of God had made God their all in all in their lives. Now he turns to you and says now we have all these witnesses, let us lay aside this weight that gets us all disturbed and makes us want to throw in the towel, and let us run with patience the race that is set before us, and let us look toward Jesus the author and finisher of our faith.

And he continued in Hebrews 12:2-3, "Looking unto Jesus the author and finisher of our faith; who for the joy that was set before him endured the cross, despising the shame, and is set down at the right hand of the throne of God. For consider him that endured such contradiction of sinners against himself, lest ye be wearied and faint in your minds." Now he is telling you how Jesus endured great afflictions, so you won't get weary in your minds.

> Hebrews 12:11-14, "Now no chastening for the present see meth to be joyous, but grievous: nevertheless afterward it yielded the peaceable fruit of righteousness unto them which are exercised thereby. Wherefore lift up the hands which hang down, and the feeble knees; And make straight paths for your feet, lest that which is lame be turned out of the way; but let it rather be healed. Follow peace with all men, and holiness, without which no man shall see the Lord."

When you join a church, make sure there's holiness there. Don't consider whether there be any popular people, professional athletes, or singers there. You ought to want to be where there is holiness. This clearly tells us that if no one lives holy, then no one will see him.

Hebrews 12:15: "Looking diligently lest any man fail of the grace of God; lest any root of bitterness springing up trouble you, and thereby many be defiled . . ." This is showing that you can fail of God's grace. Also, he is saying you can allow bitterness in your heart, for example, being upset at somebody for what they did or said to you. Before you know it, it will defile you or anyone around you. You will begin to bleed on other people about your mess. You have to take these issues to the Lord and leave them there.

Hebrews 12:16-17, ". . . Lest there be any fornicator, or profane person, as Esau, who for one morsel of meat sold his birthright. For ye know how that afterward, when he would have inherited the blessing, he was rejected: for he found no place of repentance, though he sought it carefully with tears." Here the writer of Hebrews is saying don't be like Esau, who had the blessing that was promised to him but sold his birthright for a morsel of meat.

When you make a choice to give up your spirituality for a fleshly engagement, you are actually exchanging your birthright for a fleshly engagement. Esau still tried to get the blessings of his father. He prayed and said, Bless me, my father. Why is this written to us? It's telling us we should treasure the things that God has given us and the opportunity of life.

Hebrews 10:35, "Cast not away therefore your confidence, which hath great recompence of reward." Whatever you have gone through, or whatever sin you have committed or situation you are in, for God's sake, don't throw in the towel! You might say, "Chief, I've been wrong, and I failed." Hey! Don't throw in the towel. Even though you have been bad, God can still heal a bad man. Even though you've backslidden, God can bring you back home again. Don't cast away your confidence!

Hebrews 10:36, "For ye have need of patience, that, after ye have done the will of God, ye might receive the promise." Many times, when we have blundered and done wrong, as soon as we get it right, we expect God to pour everything on us immediately. When you get it right, you have to have patience for God to bring to you those things that he has promised you, and you must endure until it comes to pass. You have to continue to be faithful until you see it unfold, and you have to believe it will happen because he said it would. He said if you ask anything in his name, he will do it. It doesn't matter how difficult it may be or how long you've been waiting, just continue trusting and believing and God will bring it to pass.

Hebrews 10:37-38, "For yet a little while, and he that shall come will come, and will not tarry. Now the just shall live by faith: but if any man draw back, my soul shall have no pleasure in him." A person who draws back is not a person walking by faith. This book illustrates what faith will do for a man, and how it will bring a man from weakness to strength, and how faith will lift up the backslider and put him back on a pedestal for God to use him again like before. Faith doesn't just deal with you where you are. Faith is something that you are looking for in the future, and that you trust will happen as you walk after God until it unfolds and brings you into the stature that God has promised you by his word. Hebrews 10:39, "But we are not of them who draw back unto perdition; but of them that believe to the saving of the soul."

Hebrews 11:1-3, "Now faith is the substance of things hoped for, the evidence of things not seen. For by it the elders obtained a good report. Through faith we understand that the worlds were framed by the Word of God, so that things which are seen were not made of things which do appear." He said worlds meaning universe, so we understand that the worlds were framed by the Word of God.

Hebrews 11:4, "By faith Abel offered unto God a more excellent sacrifice than Cain, by which he obtained witness that he was righteous, God testifying of his gifts: and by it he being dead yet speaketh." When I read that Scripture, I see that my faith is exhibited in my offerings. If you want to know how much faith God sees you have, it's when you pull out your pocketbook and pay your tithes and give your offering—that's your faith. Here is why I made this statement concerning faith.

The Bible says in Luke 6:38, "Give, and it shall be given unto you; good measure, pressed down, and shaken together, and running over, shall men give into your bosom. For with the same measure that ye mete withal it shall be measured to you again." You say you believe that, but when you have a difficult time paying your tithes, it shows that you don't believe that God is going to give that back, pressed down, shaken together, and running over. If there were a bank that promised everyone who makes a deposit that the bank would increase it and add to it, I promise you every citizen in America would start going to that bank. Now here is God who cannot lie and has made such a promise to us in our giving. So why is it that you hesitate when you give? It's because you don't believe, but you don't want to tell yourself that you don't believe.

Abel, by faith, gave God the best he had. God told his brother if you do well you will be accepted, so they both knew what was well. God had respect unto Abel's sacrifice, but unto Cain he had no regard to it. If I don't want to give in church, God has no regard to it. One thing I want you to know is that your tithe is not a gift. The Bible never said that you give tithes; the Bible says you pay tithes. For example, Abraham paid tithes and Isaac also. Tithes are something you owe unto God, not something that you're giving to God. Malachi 3:8, "Will a man rob God? Yet ye have robbed me. But ye say, Wherein have we robbed thee? In tithes and offerings." When you don't give, not only do you not have faith, but God classifies you as a robber.

We see Matthew 19:16-22, where there was a rich young ruler who asked Jesus what he must do to inherit eternal life. Jesus said, You know the commandments, so do them. So, the man asked, Which commandments? Jesus said, Do not kill, do not commit adultery, do not steal, do not bear false witness, honor your father and mother and love your neighbor as yourself. The man said, I've done that from my youth up. When Jesus heard this he said, You still lack one thing; go sell that you have and give to the poor, then come and follow me. Mark 10:21 says that Jesus looked on this man and loved him. See, you think the preacher does not love you when he tells you to pay your tithes. If this man had turned to Christ, Christ would have given back to him, pressed down, and shaken together because that is what he has already declared. Jesus said in Matthew 7:2, "and with what measure ye mete, it shall be measured to you again."

Now how many can really believe Jesus? Do you really believe Jesus, or do you doubt what Jesus says? The believer doesn't just pick out portions of what Jesus said or decide how much they want to believe but believes everything that Jesus said as he said it. We don't have the power to pick and choose how much of the Word we want to believe, because you will find yourself not picking and choosing adequately enough to serve correctly.

Hebrews 11:7, "By faith Noah, being warned of God of things not seen as yet, moved with fear, prepared an ark to the saving of his house; by the which he condemned the world, and became heir of the righteousness which is by faith." This man took on a job for one hundred twenty years, and you might spend two hours in church, and that's too long for you. What if God told you to work one hundred twenty years on a project that you weren't the biggest beneficiary of? You could get by with a canoe, but here you have to build an ark for all the animals, and it's going to take you one hundred twenty years working every day to get it done. Noah took that project and did not stop, but the Bible says he moved with fear of things not seen. See, you don't wait for things to be seen to decide how you are going to manage it and make it work out for you. That's not how faith works. True faith says: if God said it, that settles it, and I'm going to do it! My whole life has been a life of faith. Faith is ever-increasing when you're obedient to God.

Now preachers are reading and preaching about this all the time. But they are not telling you that faith is a commitment to God. Faith is your devotion to what God says. If you are not devoted to God according to God's Word, you are an unbeliever. The Bible said it like this in James 2:19-21, "Thou believest that there is one God; thou doest well: the devils also believe, and tremble. But wilt thou know, O vain man, that faith without works is dead? Was not

Abraham our father justified by works, when he had offered Isaac his son upon the altar?" So, you must trust to the point of responding to what God has said.

Peter, in the Bible, walked on the water. Matt. 14:28 reads, "And Peter answered him and said, Lord, if it be thou, bid me come unto thee on the water." The key is, don't just believe any old thing, and don't just fabricate something in your mind, but rather look in the Bible and find what God says that relates to you and believe what God says to another because he is saying the same to you. If God says unto one, then he is saying to another. Peter looked out there and said, Jesus, if that is you, tell me to walk on the water to meet you. Jesus told him to come.

It continues in Matthew 14:29-30, "And when Peter was come down out of the ship, he walked on the water, to go to Jesus. But when he saw the wind boisterous, he was afraid, and beginning to sink, he cried, saying, Lord, save me." Peter began to look at the circumstances which caused him to doubt. As a result of doubting, he began to sink, but then Jesus responded.

Matthew 14:31, "And immediately Jesus stretched forth his hand, and caught him, and said unto him, O thou of little faith, wherefore didst thou doubt?" The message in this is that when you step out on Christ's word, the Scripture says, in Psalm 37:23-24, "The steps of a good man are ordered by the Lord: and he delighteth in his way. Though he fall, he shall not be utterly cast down: for the Lord upholdeth him with his hand."

Step on out there and trust God. If you want to record a CD for the sake of the Kingdom, then record a CD. If you want to open up a daycare center so that you can bless the ministry and take care of your family, and leave an inheritance to your children's children, then seek wisdom about it and learn all about that business. Do the same for whatever you are seeking God for, and don't limit yourself to just what's in hand's reach. Start trusting for things that are beyond hand's reach. It will make you pray and will make you straighten your life up even more. These things will come to pass in your life.

The Bible says in Luke 12:32, "Fear not, little flock; for it is your Father's good pleasure to give you the kingdom." God is not walking around, not wanting to be good to his servants. He wants to show himself strong because you are the representation of him. You are the one that shows what he is in the world. God brings heaven down to the earth through our lives. But you have to trust in him.

Look what he says in Hebrews 11:8, "By faith Abraham, when he was called to go out into a place which he should after receive for an inheritance, obeyed; and he went out, not knowing whither he went." This man was called to go out, and this is the same testimony that I have of God. God called me out of a rapidly growing, flourishing church here in Houston, Texas, to Lake Charles, Louisiana, where I only had eight members. In Houston, people were beginning to know who I was, but God sent me away. I didn't know why he sent me away, but I obeyed. I went to Lake Charles, and I was rejected, but nothing stopped me because I knew who sent me. I never knew in the end that God would send me back to my hometown of Houston. I was so ready to do what he told me, that if I had to stay in Lake Charles, I was going to do that.

The Lake Charles church is now launching out, and it is the mother church of all of our churches. I placed a pastor over that church, and God sent me back to Houston by faith. See, in Lake Charles, I had a nice home and everything, but I came back to Houston and had to stay in a traveling camper. I was staying on church ground and didn't even have hot water. However, I was not looking at my condition at that moment because I knew what God had for me. God is having me tell you that he has greater things in life for you. Though I tell you about me, it is not really about me. God is looking for somebody to show himself strong in. When you get to the end of having done everything you can, and when you start trusting in him, that's when you are stronger than ever before.

Hebrews 11:8, "By faith Abraham, when he was called to go out into a place which he should after receive for an inheritance, obeyed; and he went out, not knowing whither he went." God told

Abraham to get out from among his kindred and "go to a land that I have chosen for you." God will sometimes move you away from a dead church to a spiritual church and bring you away from negative people who keep bringing you down. There are people who will grab ahold of you and try to keep you bound when you are attempting to follow after God completely. They will tell you how much they love you and don't want you to leave. When it comes to your soul, don't feel sorry for anyone. You must not allow yourself to go to hell to make someone else happy. You tell them, "Let's go get ourselves right with God." God has something good for every one of us if we come to him with our whole hearts.

Let's look at Hebrews 11:10, "For he looked for a city which hath foundations, whose builder and maker is God." Abraham looked for the city that God had made for him.

Hebrews 11:14-15, "For they that say such things declare plainly that they seek a country. And truly, if they had been mindful of that country from whence they came out, they might have had opportunity to have returned." That is a paramount Scripture. Anybody who's turning away from a lifestyle that is against God must get that stuff off your mind. Don't let people keep texting you or calling you on the phone, reminding you of stuff that you are trying to get away from. The Bible just said if you are mindful of what you came out from, and if you keep it on your mind, it will bring you back to it.

Paul said in Philippians 3:13, "Brethren, I count not myself to have apprehended: but this one thing I do, forgetting those things which are behind, and reaching forth unto those things which are before."

I want to tell you that Jesus is coming back. The Bible says in 2 Peter 3:10, "But the day of the Lord will come as a thief in the night; in the which the heavens shall pass away with a great noise, and the elements shall melt with fervent heat, the earth also and the works that are therein shall be burned up."

There are people who will say you know the earth is going to abide forever, and yes, it will. But you have to understand it will abide forever because God will continue to make a heaven and an earth. He is not saying that this earth will not be destroyed but rather that he will do it over again. It's like this—if I'm a car manufacturer and I manufacture a Honda Accord, and I say we will always have a Honda Accord, that does not mean that it will always be a 2013 model. That means whenever we make another vehicle, as long as my company exists, I will make a new car and that we will call it a Honda Accord. So, the earth will always abide, but not this identical earth.

When we stand before him, we want to hear him say, "Well done, my good and faithful servant."

Romans 12:18, "Let us with all that lieth in us live peaceably with all men."

Hebrews 10:24, "And let us consider one another to provoke unto love and to good works." What does he mean provoking unto love?

Romans 12:20-21, "Therefore if thine enemy hunger, feed him; if he thirst, give him drink: for in so doing thou shalt heap coals of fire on his head. Be not overcome of evil, but overcome evil with good."

If we have an enemy who hates us, we need to try to find a way to get some food to them. We need to understand, as we start carrying out God's Word by faith, we will see all of God's Word being fulfilled in our lives.

When I was bound by so many sinful ways and habits, I thought it was impossible for me to be saved because I understood God's Word that said "holiness without which no man shall see the Lord" (Heb. 12:14). For many years, I tried to find the true and living God. I heard many different views of the same Scriptures and found it very hard to determine what was true. I was told that there were many different interpretations of the Bible, and it was for the people to choose which one they wanted to believe in. I could never understand how God would give us His Word, yet would accept us defining it the way we wanted to. For example, in literary works such as biographies, novels, magazine or newspaper articles, the author's message is clear to the audience. It became obvious to me that the Bible as "God's Word" has a consistent and clear message that is not open to private interpretation (2 Pet. 1:20).

I have shared several examples in this book where one could preach a message using the Bible, but in reality be preaching a lie, either through intent or ignorance of the context of the Scripture. If we are to count ourselves as disciples, Jesus said, "You shall know the truth and the truth shall make you free" (John 8:32).

Printed in the USA
CPSIA information can be obtained
at www.ICGtesting.com
LVHW082026080124
768424LV00005B/449